Forty Years of
Practice

FINDING PURPOSE IN PAIN

Tezlyn Reardon

ISBN 978-1-64003-460-0 (Paperback)
ISBN 978-1-64003-461-7 (Digital)

Copyright © 2017 Tezlyn Reardon
All rights reserved
First Edition

Covenant Books, Inc.
11661 Hwy 707
Murrells Inlet, SC 29576
www.covenantbooks.com

CONTENTS

ACKNOWLEDGMENTS

After forty-one years on this beautiful, crazy, confusing, wonderful planet, I have been more than blessed to find an amazing support system through all the seasons of my life. I could write an entire book about the people who have motivated me to be and do my best, but I will start by saying thank you. If you have met me for a few minutes or for forty years, you have a purpose in my life and I thank you.

To my mother, there are not enough words in the world to even come close to describing what you mean to me. You were one half of my VIP fan club, an exclusive two-person group. I have never thought of you as just my mother; you were always a friend to me. You are an amazing woman who has taught me so many things; your selflessness and caring are unmatched by anyone I have ever met. The love and patience that you showed to dad through his cancer battle put you right up there with any cast of heroes in my book. I love you more.

To MEK, I know that although you are not here to share this moment with me in person, you are looking down, still cheering me on from the best seat in the bleachers. You have a big part in this story for so many reasons and you continue to influence my life to this day. I miss you more than I can even express, but I am so thankful for the time I had with you. And I can't wait until the day I get to see you again.

To Tyson, although you won't appreciate this when the book is published, I hope that you know what you have added to my life. I would never have imagined how much another human being could add to my life, how much love I could feel, and how proud I would be to be your mommy. I hope that I can be even a quarter of the parent to you that your gamma and papaw were to me. You are a special little boy with a family who will always have your back. I hope you know how much potential you have and that you never stop fighting, never stop dreaming, no matter what life throws at you. You are the light of my life on days when the darkness doesn't seem to end. Thank you for just being you and never, ever stop, lubby.

To the UMASS women's basketball players from 1994 to 1999, thank you just isn't enough. You were there with me for some of the gloomiest days in my life and some of the most incredible moments. We may not have always gotten along, Lord knows there was plenty of drama, but you are all my family, you all became my sisters. My fondest memories were in Amherst and I love each and every one of you, you play a huge part in my story, and this book is as much a part of you as it is a part of me, one, two, three, TOGETHER!

To Pat, I don't even know where to start. Despite where we are right now in our lives, you made the last fourteen years of my life worth living. To say we had ups and downs would be like saying the Dragster at Cedar Point is a little roller coaster. We experienced many things in our season that a lot of married couples never face. We both lost our fathers, we lived in a fifty-degree apartment for almost two years, and we survived both working third shift at the same damn time. Look at us now, writing books and running state programs! We also made a little boy that keeps us on our toes, both laughing and pulling our hair out, but I wouldn't have him any other way. He is a perfect combination of each of us and I know he has a great life ahead of him with the two of us working together. He is one lucky boy to have us as his parents; I hope he knows that! We may have screwed up a lot of things together, but he was my favorite "oops"! Thank you. Thank you for everything you have done and everything you have been. You have come so far from the first day I met you and I hope that you see all those things that I saw in you back then. I am so proud of the man and the father you have become and I was so proud to be your wife. I love you and I always will.

INTRODUCTION

In the immortal words of Allen Iverson, "Practice? We talkin' bout practice?" Sorry, AI, but yes, we talkin' bout practice. If you have no idea what I am referencing, take two minutes to Google *Allen Iverson practice* and then come back to start the book. It's well worth your time.

"I feel like I have a book inside of me." How many times have you heard someone say that they just can't see themselves having the time to write a book? Well, I have said it at least one hundred times and I have sat down to pen my life on paper at least three times, each saying, "This time is for real. I'm going to write until I can't write anymore." It's the last week of 2016 and I said in January of 2016 (the year of my fortieth birthday) that I would write three chapters of a book. It seemed realistic back then. I mean, three chapters are nothing. I've been on this earth for forty years; I could fill three chapters in my sleep. But then, life happened. In January, I didn't plan for the unplannables (yes, I'm making that a word, I'm the author, remember?) and I didn't adjust the adjustables.

Well, in all that chaos and uncertainty coupled with an unexpected diagnosis at age thirty-nine, I am trying it again. I have a story to tell. I have a pretty good story to tell. I like to think I'm a decent writer and I've been told by many people that they love to read anything I write. Granted, some of those people are talking about my posts they see on Facebook, but come on, it is THE Facebook. That's where legends are made, even if in our own minds. My fortieth year didn't go as I had planned, but let's be honest, neither did the first thirty-nine.

2016 was supposed to be my year of defining and refining, the year I threw caution to the wind and just did it, thanks to Nike for that overused cliché. I was going to set the world on fire and no one would be able to tell me anything, let alone keep up with the pace of my worldwide adventures. It sounded good, in theory. In reality, it was probably the hardest year of my life. Oh, it was defining, alright; be careful what you wish for. I thought I had already overcome the big things in my life and that maybe I was finally able to put it into cruise control and sit back and enjoy the ride. Apparently, someone forgot to tell me that you don't put your car on cruise control on the Autobahn that I called my "forty in forty" year.

Those who know me know that I was defined for a large portion of my life by my athletic ability. From hitting home runs in tee ball to breaking noses in volleyball (yeah, that really happened) to winning basketball games by fifty points in high school, I was Tez, the athlete. This continues to this day, even though I can barely walk, let alone think about jumping or running. If I know one thing really well, I know sports. I even majored in sport management, shocking, huh? It has been a huge part of my life for thirty-five years, and even though I am not able to do what I once was really good at, I enjoy being around sports and watching sports and talking sports with anyone and everyone who will listen and argue with me. So, it just made sense that I write a book about my life that has a sports title. At first, it seemed corny and predictable, but then I realized it's who I am. Why shouldn't I write a book with a sports theme in the title? It's probably damn near expected for me to write it.

My life has literally been a game. Everything in life is a game. Everyone wants to win; no one wants to lose. Whether it be a football game, a scrabble game, or a job interview, everyone wants to say, "I WIN! Who's got next?" Who doesn't want to hear the roar of the crowd shouting your name when you hit a game-winning shot or give a million-dollar presentation for new business? If you said, "Not me," then please put this book down right now and give it to someone else. You won't understand. For those of you who are like me and race people off the line at a stop light, every single time, then keep reading. I think you'll be able to get inside my head (that's frightening and fascinating at the same time) and replay your own practice or game in your mind. If it helps, imagine Jay Bilas in your head providing color commentary about my life. He will be the narrator to my life story when it hits the movie theaters; you just watch.

Let's do this.

CHAPTER 1

Small-Town Girl, Big-Time Dreams

Practice started a looooong time ago, January 9, 1976, to be exact. There was no three-point line. There was no Instagram or Facebook or YouTube to replay sick dunks over and over. The basketball shorts players wore were what the kids nowadays call "nut huggers." Back then, I would have had to write this story on soft handwriting paper with a big fat blue pencil that won't fit in any pencil sharpener. Am I dating myself too much? Okay, so forty years isn't so bad, but I have seen so many changes in the world and in my own life in that time. If I were to go back to 1976 and tell my parents what I would be writing about today, I think they would have told you to go smoke whatever it is they smoked back then or my dad might have taken you to the Home Tavern for a beer to have a good laugh with his friends. If I remember the story correctly, I was a miracle baby. My mom only had one ovary and she didn't think she could have kids. Well, if this isn't one hell of a way to start my life. That should give you some indication as to what the rest of my life would hold. I'm not one to be told I can't do something. She also thought she was having a boy. So of course I was a girl because I had to prove everyone wrong!

From a very early age, I was introduced to sports. My mom played women's softball and traveled all over the state of Ohio on teams with my aunts and some of the best female athletes to come out of Southeastern Ohio. Crazy how long it took to get the first female athlete into the Logan High School Athletic Hall of Fame, but that's for another book! She played volleyball and also bowled in two to three leagues. My mom was kind of a celebrity; she was on a show called "Bowl for Dollars" when I was younger. Okay, well, maybe she was a celebrity to me. Anyway, I came from a family of athletes, on both sides of my family. Including myself, there are six members of my family in the LHS Hall of Fame and another one that should be in there. It was in my blood and it was never a question if I would play sports; it was just when and which ones.

I'm going to let you in on a little secret now, so that you're not shocked by it later and completely miss very important details of my story. I am an Oreo and I'm proud to call myself an Oreo. If you don't know, I'm half-black and half-white. In grade school, I checked "Other" when I filled out testing forms because I had no idea what I was and you were only allowed to pick one! I would much rather tell someone what to call me rather than them coming up with something on their own that isn't quite as "cute." And everyone loves Oreos, so why not? Some think I'm wrong for calling myself that, but I like to think it's endearing. If I'm not offended by it, you shouldn't be either. I'm not one for political correctness, but I am one for making fun of myself, especially if it makes someone else uncomfortable! You can call me an asshole, I like to say I'm enjoying life.

I started with soccer in kindergarten; it was the only thing available at that age back then. But let me tell ya, if you had tried to predict my athletic career based on soccer, you would have guessed I would be in the band. It's not that there's anything wrong with band, just that that would have been the only way I would have made it onto any sports field; that's all I'm saying. Anyway, I was the one running around the field picking flowers or playing in the dirt. My coach stuck me back in the goal thinking that would help keep me still. Nope. I was the kid swinging on the crossbar, still playing in the dirt, wrapping myself up in the net, waving at my friends getting ready for the next game. I'm guessing I probably had a few goals scored against me. But as time went on, I was able to start in tee ball softball, where I was a little better. I started playing the outfield and, well, soccer Tez came back and I was in the dirt and grass. One of my teammates broke her collarbone and they moved me to pitcher. At pitcher, even in tee ball, you have to pay attention or you can catch a line drive right in the kisser. In my first game, I can remember a line drive coming back at me, going right toward the face of the umpire behind me. I stuck my glove up just at the right time, I might have even closed my eyes, and I saved her some money in plastic surgery costs! The rest is history. I don't think I ever played any position but pitcher from that point up through pony league softball. My mom was a pitcher, so I think she was happy about that transition.

Once junior high started, I was introduced to volleyball. But, let's be clear; it is nothing like the kids playing volleyball these days where they start club ball in fourth grade. Oh no, we played bump ball: Serve the ball. Bump the ball back over. Bump the ball back over. Bump the ball back over. Yeah, it was really exciting. I wasn't even good enough to serve the ball overhand, I had to serve side-armed, and that's not even a thing. We played on team, Chillicothe Smith, who actually used all three hits when the ball was served to them! We thought they were the Olympic team the way they would bump-set-spike and we would be happy just to get a hand on the ball before it hit the floor. As the years went on, Chillicothe became one of our out-of-league rivals and we had some pretty heated battles. We gave them our best, but we just never had their number. However, we evened the score in basketball season.

I didn't start playing basketball until I was in fifth grade in a very rare girl's-only basketball league. Even being in a small town, we had a lot of supportive and hardworking adults who wanted to bring as many opportunities for kids to town as they could, probably to keep us out of trouble. From that league, I was chosen to be on a traveling team called the Logan Wildcats. There was just one thing about this team and the games we would play. We played against all-boy's teams. Imagine the boys walking in the gym for the first team to see ten girls in the layup line at the opposite end of the court, laughing and wondering why their coach is making them play against some dumb girls. Well, they weren't laughing by the end of the game. I'm not sure of our record and how we finished, but each year, we were always in the hunt for the championship and we beat every team at least, except the Logan Comets. We just couldn't beat them and some of my best guy friends were on that team, which made it that much worse. Some of them still don't let us live it down, but one of our teams went to the OHSAA state championship game in 1992 and the other didn't. I'll let you guess which one.

In my high school career, our basketball teams from my freshman year to my senior year were 94-10 with a trip to the state semifinals, another to the state championship game, 2 regional runner-ups, and 4 SEOAL league championships. We were good. We were really good. In our first game in seventh grade, we beat a team 88-7. They weren't much closer even when we got to high school. In my class, we had "the three freshmen" who were on varsity our very first year of high school. It was rare for a freshman to get any substantial playing time, let alone three. We were paired with one of the best American women's basketball players ever to play the game, Katie Smith (just Google her; I'm sure you've heard of her!). We couldn't be touched in Southeastern Ohio. Some thought we could beat just about any boys' team and some thought we could have given the Ohio State women's team a run for their money. I know, people around here also think the Ohio State football team could beat the Cleveland Browns, but hey, we are passionate about our sports in Ohio.

Early on in my high school career, my dad and I talked over and over about my chance to play basketball in college. Would I be able to play Division I? Could I dare dream of playing overseas? I played on an extremely talented AAU team during the summer and we went to four AAU national tournaments, finishing as high as fifth in the nation. We had eight people from that team continue their playing careers at a Division I university and very well, I might add. I made the decision to attend the University of Massachusetts, much to the dismay of my mother who wanted me to go to Cincinnati or Ohio University and stay in the state. That was the biggest decision in my eighteen years and it was a difficult one. It was then that I realized in order for me to be successful and grow, I had to get out of my comfort zone and be on my own.

Okay, so I think I might have skipped through high school a little too quickly. If I stop and think about some of the things I have done and learned from in my fortyish years, I'm guessing that a lot of it was rooted in my teenage years. I would love to say I was the most popular girl with the perfect curly brown hair and the cute little figure that all the guys fell all over just to get to talk to. Actually, I'm kind of glad that I'm not going to say that because I'm not sure I would be where I am today if that were the case. Hey, it's my book; I can say whatever I want!

On the contrary, I was popular among my guy friends, but not for the reasons you think a girl would be popular in younger years. Don't get me wrong, I was the girl that was always picked first, in gym class or on the playground. If games of dodgeball and flag football were counted as boyfriends or dates, girl, I would have been the class hussy. I could run faster, hit the ball harder, and jump higher than most girls in the school and probably more than some guys. But, as you can probably guess, that wasn't a desired trait of a girl you wanted to date. Sure, I spent lots of time talking about football and March Madness with the guys in study hall or at lunch, but I was never the first one called for a date to the dance or prom or even a movie.

I would say I was a little awkward in high school or maybe I was just misunderstood. Obviously more than once, I had people tell me they thought I was a lesbian in high school because I played sports, but, honestly, I was in love with sports. I scheduled my life around AAU tournaments and basketball games on TV or Ohio State basketball games with my dad. I was a goody two-shoes; I didn't want to get in any trouble EVER because I was afraid I would have to miss a game or a practice and that just wasn't an option. While my friends were out on dates and drinking at house parties or bonfires, I was probably at home watching a game on TV or getting ready for a track meet the next day. In some ways, it was a choice, but in some ways, it was a coping mechanism because there were many nights I didn't have anyone to "cruise town" with because all my friends were with their boyfriends and I, well, I wasn't. I remember quite a few nights that I would sit at home and cry because I just wanted someone to hang out and watch games with or go to the movies with. Hell, I just wanted someone to want to hang out with ME.

Picture if you will a skinny, 5' 10", 120 lbs (my name became the splendid splinter on the local radio broadcasts) girl with curly brown hair. That doesn't sound so bad, right? For a better visualization, another nickname was Chia Pet, one of those "sold on television" gimmicks that you spread the seed mixture on the clay pot with the creepy face and watch the weeds grow from its head. I was skinny, almost too skinny, and I had a large, puffy afro that would have made JJ Walker jealous! There was a time when afros were the bomb diggity and people would have killed to have my precious curly locks. But this was the early 1990s, not the 1970s. I was teased and pestered at school, but I took it as friendly ribbing, just having a good time. But at opposing high schools, it was way worse and not so friendly. I was called everything from a half-breed to a freak of nature and there I can recall a few chants of "AFRO, AFRO" as I shot free throws. Thankfully, in those latter situations, my game made up for my hairstyle and I usually was on the winning end with the "SCOREBOARD, SCOREBOARD" chant. But the wins didn't make the tears go away. Hocking County was one of the whitest counties in the state of Ohio and every person of color was either my family or they were married into my family. I couldn't wait to go to college and be around other people "like me."

CHAPTER 2

We're Not in Kansas Anymore

September 1994, Amherst, Massachusetts, is a ten-hour drive. That's how long I had to think about what I was about to do. The further I got from home, the harder it would be to tell my dad to turn the car around and drive like the wind back to Logan, Ohio! Sure, in theory, moving away from home to spread my wings and make a name for myself sounded great back in November when I signed my National Letter of Intent to play basketball at UMASS. But now, with each mile, each stop at a gas station along I-90, each change of the music in my CD player, this felt like the biggest mistake of my life. What if I don't like my roommate? What if I don't like my coach? What if I don't like my teammates? What if they don't like me? Was I really good enough to play at a Division I college? Should I have just gone to Ohio University so I could run home every night after practice or class if I needed a good cry on mom's shoulder? What the HELL am I doing?

I saw my dad cry for one of the few times I ever saw him get choked up in my first eighteen years. The funny thing is I think he cried in front of me, while my mom waited until they got in the car to drive away. Imagine that, my mom comforting my dad when just months earlier she was ready to give me up for adoption at the age of seventeen because I chose to go to school seven hundred miles away! Talk about the twilight zone!

Remember that skinny 5' 10", 120 lbs girl I talked about? Well, just 2 short months later, that girl was replaced by a 150 lbs, muscular, healthy-looking, physically fit college basketball player with muscles she never knew existed. She knew they were there now, because she could see them. And, frankly, they hurt. When they say high school is nothing like college, please believe they are telling the truth, in more ways than one. I ran more my first month of preseason my freshman year than I did my entire high school athletic career, including track season! We had to complete a one-and-a-half-mile run in eleven minutes before we were able to move inside to the court to continue the torture on the hardwood instead of the smelly rubber, "Code Red," as we so affectionately referred to her. Should have been easy for someone who ran track for six years, right? Oh, hell no. It took me 5 times to get it right, and even then, I think our assistant coach cheated for me because she was tired at getting up at 6:00 a.m. to time me every day! Needless to say, that wasn't the only hard lesson I was going to learn over the next few months and years.

I could write an entire book about my five-year college career, and I sincerely might someday, but I am going to stick with the defining moments to keep this book moving along. Trust me, I won't leave you disappointed; there is a lot to cover!

My freshman and sophomore years brought a lot of growing pains on the court, in the classroom, in my friendships, and in my body. I had a decent preseason my freshman year and I was name an A-10 conference "Freshman of Influence" before I even stepped on campus. I played with Ohio State/ABL/WNBA/Olympic all-everything basketball player Katie Smith in high school; apparently, they thought that she had the golden touch and I was supposed to be just like her simply by playing next to her for two years. Lord, I wish it worked that way! I was pretty good in my own right, but there is a reason that Katie retired from the WNBA as the leading scorer in the HISTORY of American professional women's basketball. Yeah, that's right, from Logan, Ohio. Who knew?

I came to UMASS with some expectations and I had some teammates who had their own expectations of me. It was an up and coming team with a great nucleus of returning players and a fiery head coach who was primed to take this program to someplace it had never been. I was to be a big part of that next step, no pressure at all. I had played behind Katie for two years in high school, so I was used to waiting patiently for the changing of the guard while learning all I could in the process. But wait, you want me to start my first two college games EVER? And it's on the road at the University of Kentucky. Okay, sure, no problem. I would love to tell you that I tore it up and never looked back and became the answer to everyone's dreams for the women's basketball program. I would really love to tell you that, but of course, this book wouldn't be very suspenseful if that's where I ended. I struggled; I struggled badly. I was driving the struggle bus to struggle land and there were no brakes on this struggle bus. I must have called home at least one hundred times crying to my mom and dad that my coach hated me, my teammates hated me, I hated basketball, and I wanted to come home. My dad put me in my place when instead of saying, "Sure, we will jump in the car and drive ten hours to come pick you up and drive another ten hours back home. See you in a few hours!" he actually said, "Well, what did you do wrong?" Huh? Are you serious? What did I do wrong? Did you just hear what I said? I am an only child, so of course I never did anything wrong; it was everyone else that had the problem. But my dad, the guy that told me I could play basketball at a Division 1 school and that I should follow my heart and go to the other side of the earth to play basketball, was now basically telling me to suck it up, stop being a spoiled brat, and do what you're told. Talk about a reality check. I thought my dad had my back. I was convinced that he and my coach were in cahoots and they were plotting against me to see how much they could torture me before I finally decided to break. Thankfully, that day never came, although it certainly could have.

Fast forward to my sophomore year, I had the best summer of my life, was in the best shape of my life, and was ready to pick up where I left off at the end of my freshman year. After a rough start to my first collegiate basketball season, I wound up figuring it out by earning my starting position back and opening the eyes of my teammates, my coaches, other teams in the league, and even myself. About seven games into the season, we flew to the University of

Florida for a four-team tournament where we would play the Gators on their home court in the first round, talk about a crazy atmosphere! Once again, I had earned a starting spot after a fourteen-point, team leading performance in a major upset of fifth-ranked Stanford. We lost to the Gators and future WNBA all-star and Olympian, DeLisha Milton and then came back the next night to beat a strong Boston College team. The team was playing the best we ever had, everything was clicking, and we looked unstoppable at times. Man, if any team caught us on the right night, we could beat anyone, just ask Stanford.

January 1, 1996, yes, I remember the day; and no, I will never forget the moment my entire college career flashed before my eyes. I won't even try to make it dramatic because I'm not sure there is any need for drama or any fancy words to describe what had happened. If I close my eyes and focus enough, I can probably still hear the pop and feel the sting of pain. We were doing a rebounding drill and I had just blocked out the best rebounder on our team and took off after the ball. The last thing I heard was my coach telling, "GO GET IT!" The next thing I heard was a pop. *No, a POP. OK, a **POP!*** And then I heard this blood curdling, train track screeching, sound that I had never heard in my life. And then, I realized I was the one screaming, worst pain ever. I swear I thought I was dying and then I wanted to pass out or throw up. I went to Springfield with my head coach for an MRI and I knew it was probably pretty serious. I was hoping for a sprained knee that would take a week or two to heal, but deep down I knew that Joanie probably wouldn't have been there with me if it was just a sprain. Joanie had her own history of knee injuries from her college-playing days at Penn State and there was only one injury that she was particularly sympathetic toward, torn ACLs. If you rolled your ankle, you better get up and put some tape on it and get your ass back on that court. If you tore your ACL, you got a little bit more of a pass and a pat on the knee as she walked out of the training room before practice.

We boarded the bus for a road trip to Philly to play Temple and our pseudo-rival, St. Joe's. I brought along a few new traveling companions with crutches and a cryo-cuff for the five-hour bus ride. After practice, my athletic trainer said she had the results and she would stop by my room when we got back to the hotel. She did, and so did Joanie. I'm sure the blood probably drained out my face when Joanie walked in and I already knew the diagnosis before they could even say the words. But it wasn't just something simple. Where was the fun in that? Imagine being in a car accident and then going to the repair shop to get an estimate. The mechanic tells you that you smashed the front of your car pretty good, but it can be fixed. Whew, that's a relief, a little setback, but recoverable. Oh, but wait. Once they got under the hood, they discovered you also have two bent axle rods, a busted radiator, and the airbag deployed; at this point, you might just have to total the car and call yourself lucky. But hey, you're still alive, so it can't be all bad. Well, I hit the trifecta + 1. I tore my ACL, MCL, PCL, and LCL. If there was a CL, chances are I tore it. I started to think they were just making up letters to tell me that I was jacked up and my college career was going to get a whole lot tougher.

So, you know how I usually start out by saying, "I'd like to tell you that . . ." when I really want to make myself look so much better than I really was? Well, I'd like to tell you that when I went to college, I evolved miraculously into this model student who attended every class, sat in the front row diligently scribbling notes and bits of priceless knowledge from each of my professors, and aced every exam because I enjoyed and embraced the college experience. I mean, after all, it is my book about my life and I could just lie about everything and lead you to believe that I am perfect in every way. But, I am far from perfect and I want others to learn from my lessons and see how my mistakes have actually shaped who I have become, in the hopes that I can help just one person realize that one mistake or two mistakes or one hundred mistakes do not a person make. You can come back from the depths of the biggest hole anyone in the history of the world has ever dug themselves into. Honestly, it takes just as much work to dig that hole in the first place as it does to dig yourself out of it. The sooner you realize that you are the one holding the shovel, the sooner you will begin using that same shovel for good rather than digging your way to China with the same mistakes over and over and over.

Up until this point, the worst injury I had ever had was a busted chin which required three stitches that I sustained while trying to do something stupid in volleyball practice. Remember that reap what you sow piece? Well, I apparently was planting stupid weed that day and I cracked my chin on the floor trying to be a superstar octopus by going after two balls in the opposite direction at the same time. Hey, I said I was athletic; I never said I was smart! Anyway, I also had a scope of my knee to remove joint mice when I was a sophomore after I somehow fractured a small part of my kneecap and the pieces were just floating around and getting stuck in places they shouldn't have been. A forty-five-minute surgery and ten days later, I was back on the track, so it wasn't really a serious injury, to me. But this injury was about to send me to a place I had never been before and make me question if I would ever be able to make it back.

I had reconstructive ACL surgery on my left knee the day before my twentieth birthday. Happy birthday to you, here are some crutches, some staples in your knee, and some pain meds. Try not to hurt yourself again. Gee, thanks. From this point on, my life was never going to be the same, in just about every way possible. I thought the excruciating pain I felt when I laid on the court just seven days earlier would be the worst part of this story, but trust me when I say the worst was still yet to come.

CHAPTER 3

Rehabbed, Rejuvenated, Reunited

One of the hardest things to do was watch my teammates, day in and day out, playing their hearts out to achieve the goal we had set for ourselves, to be in contention for the A-10 title and to make the NCAA tournament. I wanted to be out there with them. I still had to prove to them that I belonged and that they could count on me to help take us to the promise land where no other women's team in UMASS basketball history had ever been. That was why I signed to play there. That is why I drove ten hours from home and left my friends and family behind, because I wanted to be part of a legacy. I wanted to build a program and be able to walk away saying, "I did that." It wasn't long after the surgery that depression set in. I couldn't play. My grades weren't as bad as my freshman year (notice how I cleverly skated by that part of my freshman year?), but they were far from great, and if I hadn't been on the basketball team, I might have been sent on a ten-hour car ride back home with no return expected. I had lost my way. All I had ever known my entire life was sports and now it was taken away from me. My body, my mind, and my soul were in a severe state of shock. It had taken almost my entire freshman season to feel like part of the team, and now, just nine games into my sophomore season, it was ripped out of my hands. I didn't rehab my knee as much as I should have because, well, it hurt. I never had to work hard at anything physically in my first twenty years; this should be a piece of cake. After my knee didn't progress the way it should have, I went in about a month later to clean out scar tissue so that I can get full range of motion and extension in my knee. I'm already up to surgery number three on my left knee, for those of you keeping score at home.

Along with depression of not being able to play, not being engaged in my academics, and feeling isolated from my teammates, I also still had this underlying incomplete feeling because I still hadn't found someone who wanted to spend time with me as more than just a friend. I figured on a campus of seventeen thousand people with about fifty percent males, there had to be someone who thought I was worth getting to know on a more personal level. With the hours spent in the classroom, on the road, at practice, in study hall, and in the weight room, I just hadn't put myself out there to meet people like I should have and I suffered because of it. While I would go out with my teammates on some weekends, there were also weekends that I sat in my dorm room alone because I just didn't want to go anywhere and I didn't have anyone to go with even if I did want to go out. As I mentioned before, I could write for days about my college experiences, but that's not what this book is centered. I will, however, tell you that I questioned my sexuality for the majority of my college years. I was confused by everything around me and I assumed that because I hadn't found a boyfriend, I must be gay. That was the only logical explanation to me, and when I started hanging out with other women on a 24/7/365 basis and found someone who paid attention to me and wanted to spend time alone with me, it didn't matter to me what gender this person was. I just wanted to be wanted. I think we all have felt that way at some point in our lives whether it be in a relationship, career, and friendships. We need to be wanted. I'm not sure if this drove me further into my depression or if the depression drove me into this thinking because of everything else I was missing, but I was not in a good place for much of my sophomore and my (first) junior year. My mom was worried about me. My friends were worried about me. Hell, I was worried about me! I was never suicidal and those thoughts never crossed my mind, but I fell into a pretty deep depression and I wasn't sure if I could mentally come back to finish my basketball career, let alone physically. This was way more

than I had ever dealt with in my life. You could say I was probably a little sheltered growing up in rural Logan, Ohio, population
nine thousand-ish depending on who you asked. I wasn't equipped
to handle this much adversity, but that didn't stop it from coming.

The summer of 1996 I spent in Logan not only getting my knee
back into shape but also getting my mind back into shape. I started
playing pickup basketball at the Central Elementary School courts
four nights a week with the guys as soon as I got home. Remember,
I had just had two knee surgeries in January and this was May/June;
I hadn't been cleared to do any playing of any kind. This is what real
authors might like to call foreshadowing. At the end of the summer
when I went back to Amherst, I was in the best shape of my life. I was
playing well. My knee felt great. This was going to be my comeback
year. That was until I started having a sharp pain in my right leg just
below my knee. I played through it, tried to ice it, massaged it, and
ibuprofen it away, but it just wouldn't get better. Come to find out,
all the playing I did on the concrete courts of Central Elementary for
about four hours a day wasn't a good thing after all. I now had a stress
fracture in my right tibia that would put me out of commission for
about six to eight weeks. Seriously? You're kidding me, right? Back
to the crutches, I went and back on the damn stationary bike that I
had gotten to know so well in my rehab with my knee. I will spare
you all of the details between that time and eight weeks later when I
was cleared to practice again. I came straight from the doctor's office
into practice, got my gear on, and ran out on the court ready to get
this comeback on track and salvage as much of this season as I could.
Forty-five minutes into my first official practice in almost a year, I
was doing a defensive drill and I made a hard push off my right foot
to the left to guard one of my teammates. I felt a pop, not like that
pop when I tore all my CLs, but one that was uncomfortable and
made my knee start to feel a little warm. I walked off to the side of
the court to shake it off and get my bearings back while my trainer
came to check on me. She asked what happened and I told her I was
fine and that I just had a catch in my knee that I needed to work out.
She said, "Run." I looked at her like she had ten heads, but she was
used to me looking at her like that. She said, "Run down to the other

end and come back." I looked down the court to get ready to trot to the other end. Instead, I turned around and headed to the training room without so much as a jog or a word. I knew I was done.

If there were ever a time to quit, this was it. All those people who told me to keep my head up and stay strong after my initial injury were now looking at me like, wow, maybe this isn't meant to be. Maybe you need to hang it up and try underwater basket weaving or something. (You know, I never did find that class as UMASS. I thought it was a pre-req for all athletes, but I guess it must have been full when I was there.) (So, yeah, depression, yada, yada, yada, surgery number four, yada, yada, yada, still can't play, yada, yada, yada.) It sounds like a broken record at this point and I almost gave up. I don't think anyone would have judged me in the slightest if I had walked into my coach's office and told her I was quitting the team and moving back home. Not many people can go through a tale like this and live to tell about it. Okay, so I didn't go off to war and I hadn't suffered some great tragedy, but I had lost a large piece of my identity once again and this time, I didn't know if I wanted it back. I did a lot of soul searching with the help of a counselor, my parents, some very good friends (they know who they are), and a few (or twelve) Bud Light.

I was never a religious person, although I grew up going to church with my grandmother until I was about fourteen. But it's amazing how religious you become when you realize nothing in your life is going as you had planned and you had to find an explanation, any explanation for why things happen to you. I also prayed a lot to the "porcelain God" my first two years of college, but I don't remember most of those conversations, nor do I want to! Over the course of my almost two-year battle with injuries, I came to live by the creed "everything happens for a reason." I didn't really know what it meant at the time, but it sounded good and I needed all the motivation I could get to keep myself from completely losing my sanity and my scholarship! When I signed to play basketball at UMASS, I was excited to help build a program and make a name for myself, which would hopefully pay off with a professional basketball career overseas. At this point, I was just hoping to be able to walk again, let alone play basketball at a high level.

Thankfully it was another adage that rang true in the summer of 1997, "Third time's a charm." After two false starts to recover my basketball career, this time, I finally took it a little (okay, a lot!) more seriously, on and off the court. I was selected to participate in Haigis Hoopla, an annual three-on-three basketball tournament hosted and organized by undergrad and graduate students in sport management. It was a big deal to be selected and it helped to take my mind off some of the other things that weren't going so well. As a side note, many of my classmates from the Haigis project are having some amazing careers, including working with the NBA, a regular female broadcaster on ESPN, a few lawyers, and one guy who gets to make videos with high-profile athletes and graces red carpets all over the place. UMASS was one of the first sport management programs in the country and is still known as one of the best, proven by the long list of graduates in each of the four major professional sports organizations and collegiate athletics.

During the spring and summer after I recovered from my latest knee surgery, I worked my butt off to make sure that once I got back on that court, it would take a herd of elephants to get me away from it again! I had one friend in particular who was with me through each and every tear, each and every bead of sweat for my entire five-year career. There weren't many people who could get more out of me than Tommy did. (Hey, Tommy, you made the book!) Tommy and I had a lot in common including R&B music (I can't count how many mix tapes we made together!), the love of basketball, and our super-duper senior years at UMASS! I was able to get out before him, but I know he was put in my life for a reason and I never would have made it without him. He would call me first thing in the morning to see what time we were going to play pickup or to shoot around at the cage. I had the keys to get into our practice facility so we could play whenever we wanted, with whomever we wanted, as long as we wanted, rain or shine, day or night. I was in the best shape of my life, physically and emotionally. My knee felt great and my shot was coming back. I could run the fast break with Tommy, and anyone who has ever played with him knows that if you can't keep up with him, you aren't getting the ball! My mind was getting back to a place where I not only felt comfortable on the court that I wasn't going to get hurt, but I also felt confident about my life and where I was headed. I was actually looking forward to preseason conditioning because for the first time, I knew I was going to make my expected mile and a half time in my first attempt. I wasn't going to have to get up at 6 a.m. until I made my time; those days were over.

I wouldn't say that the season started out in a blaze of glory, with me in the starting lineup, leading every offensive category. Notice I said "offensive" because if anyone reading this knows anything about me, defense wasn't exactly my specialty. What can I say, I knew my role! It took me a few games to get back into the swing of things, and that is an understatement. It literally was like learning to walk all over again. With each step I took, I was worried that someone would step on my foot or there would be a scene straight out of *The Birds* with ravenous birds coming from everywhere, attacking my left knee like it was fresh roadkill on a sunny day in the middle of nowhere. No, really, I was terrified I would do it again. I can't count how many times my coach told me to get off the court if I couldn't play full speed and to quit worrying about my knee. It took a while, but once it started to click, it was a whole new ballgame.

By the end of the 1997–1998 season, the team had found our rhythm and I was finally playing the type of basketball that had been expected from me when I was recruited back in high school. We had a run of about eleven or twelve wins to wind up the regular-season Atlantic 10 Eastern Conference champions and we hosted the Atlantic 10 tournament for the first time ever. Despite losing a gut-wrenching overtime championship game to Virginia Tech, I was named tournament Most Outstanding Player and we were headed to the NCAA tournament in Iowa City, Iowa. We lost that game in Iowa, but I had one of the more memorably halves of my shortened career with eighteen points in the first half. I felt as if everything that left my hand was destined to go in the hoop. It's what players call being "in the zone" and I was in it. I was named second team All Atlantic 10 Conference, earning the first official accolades of my

FORTY YEARS OF PRACTICE

career that didn't involve the number of consecutive games missed due to injury.

After the Atlantic 10 tournament in Amherst, which my parents had driven up for, I saw that emotion from my father that I had when they dropped me off for the first time. A man of few words, he hugged me tightly and said, "You came a long way, kid," and that was better than any trophy or award that I ever could have received. He knew that I worked hard to get where I was and this was what we had talked about on all those random road trips through the country. I was living out a dream, although I think he knew all along what I was capable of; I just needed to see it for myself.

There was a legendary coach at UMASS in the 1970s who coached a guy by the name of Julius Erving; you might have heard of him a few times. His name was Jack Leaman, and if they made an audio recording of the embodiment of a true Bostonian accent, Jack would be on the top of my list, hands down. Jack had remained around campus following his coaching career with Dr. J and helped coach the women's team prior to my arrival, as well as the agricultural college team, Stockbridge, and he provided the very colorful commentary on the local radio broadcast for basketball games. When I first met Jack on my recruiting trip, he almost knocked me down the hill we were standing on because he gave me the biggest hug I have ever received, and at 120 lbs, I was not ready for what he was about to dish out! He was so supportive of our team and always had some words of encouragement, no matter how bad you played, but he would tell you that, too. Jack affectionately referred to me as an "institution." This was coming from a guy who had been on campus before. But I knew he meant it with the utmost respect and adoration, and I accepted my rightful moniker with good humor as it was intended. We lost Jack in 2004, but I will never forget that smile, that laugh, that hug, that "institution."

This leads me to what I lovingly call my "second senior year." We had high hopes after finishing the previous season strong, despite a short stay in the NCAA tournament. We had all but two of our key players from the previous year returning and another who was making her comeback after a torn ACL. We had two incoming freshmen and two transfers who were eligible to make their debut for us that season. Unfortunately, the season started off with controversy before we hit the court for our first game. During our first team meeting in the preseason, we all committed to making basketball our priority and we were willing to make tough decisions if we found out players were not holding up their end of the bargain. Without going into too many details, one player was dismissed from the team for a violation of team rules and two others quit because they felt the punishment did not fit the crime. From there, the season spiraled out of control, and we never could get back to the team we thought we could be. A lawsuit was filed by the former players against our coach and we all were affected by it, on and off the court. It was never a choice that we wanted to make against one of our own, but we thought we were doing the right thing at the time.

We ended that dreary, emotionally draining season with a 16-14 record, nowhere near the dream season we were hoping for. I was named second team all-conference and scored my one thousandth point a week after my twenty-third birthday in a game against Temple in Amherst. My parents were not able to make it for that game as it was during the week and the following weekend we would be in Ohio for my final college game in my home state. Thankfully they were able to hear the game being broadcasted on the radio station through this crazy new thing called the World Wide Web. The date of that achievement was January 16, 1999. You are going to want to remember that date, as it will become even more significant in another season of my life.

Chapter 4

Now What?

You remember the story of the *Tortoise and the Hare*, right? How that cocky, self-absorbed rabbit was so sure of himself beating that lowly, outmatched turtle that he was stopping to kiss the girls on the race trail, slowing down to play a game of spades with the fellas on the corner, and even having time to lay down for a nap before crossing the finish line? He was pretty confident that he had everything under control and there was nothing that could stop him. That was me graduating from college. I grabbed my diploma, hopped in my car, and drove as fast as I could back to Logan, Ohio, to begin this new amazing life that was just going to be given to me because, well, I earned it, right? I had the degree, and finding a job should be easy. I also had an agent, so it would only be a matter of time before I would get the call to pack my bags and head off to play professional basketball overseas. This was the beginning of the rest of my life. The sky is the limit; no one can stop me. I felt like I had just whooped my opponent in the game of life, so I can take my foot off the gas and cruise a little bit, take a break, relax, and enjoy the ride. I think someone forgot to tell my parents that because, get this, they wanted me to get a job and start paying my own bills. I know, right? Don't you remember, I just won the Atlantic 10 tournament MVP a few short months ago? I don't need a job. I deserve to rest because I had a tough five years in college and I can't be expected to get a job right away. Besides, my phone will be ringing very soon to go play basketball;

that's my job. In sports, there are these things called lockouts. Fans don't like lockouts because it means they don't get to watch any games while the players and teams are arguing over the difference between a $21 million contract and a $21.1 million contract. Veteran players don't mind lockouts because they get to take a few extra weeks of rest or vacation and still get fat stacks of cash while they do it. Players who would be rookies don't like lockouts because all tryouts are on hold or canceled until the lockout is over. My senior year there was a lockout in the WNBA while they were negotiating the first collective bargaining agreement in women's professional basketball and all tryouts were canceled. I was crushed because I had a tryout with the Detroit Shock and Coach Nancy Lieberman-Cline who I had met at a professional development camp a few months earlier. She told me at the end of that camp that if I got myself into the best shape of my life, I would set myself apart from the other attendees and I would make her team. Money in the bank, I got this. Yeah, that tryout never happened, and all of those positions overseas that I was waiting on were filled by other graduating seniors with much more impressive accolades and pedigree than I and there were also still many veteran ABL players who hadn't migrated to the WNBA that were now playing overseas. Now what?

During my junior year, the harsh reality hit that I had to go to class and study in order to graduate from college. I didn't have basketball in my life for almost two years, so I had plenty of time to do what I was there to do in the first place, getting my degree. As a matter of fact, I left with two. I was able to get through those injuries and other struggles because I believed there had to be something or someone bigger at work in my life, or at least that's what I told myself to stay motivated and looking forward in my life. If I hadn't done that, I'm not so sure I would be writing these words right now. The only thing that I didn't take advantage of during that time, and if there was ever a regret in my life this would be it, was taking the summer to participate in an internship. I spent my summers getting back in shape so that I could get back on the court. Aside from taking a few summer classes to catch up or get ahead, I really wasn't focused on the years after college, just getting back what I had taken away from me. In a sense, I ended up taking away future career opportunities, but I wouldn't know that until many years later.

Once I moved back home after graduation, attended my five-year high school class reunion, and enjoyed a summer of catching up with friends, which included catching up on any alcoholic beverage that I might have missed over the last two years, I decided (okay, my parents decided) it was time to get a job. I majored in sport management with a double major in creative writing/marketing, but there was nothing in Logan, Ohio, that was going to be anywhere near those two areas. In Logan, you are either a teacher or a nurse, you work in one of the few factories that are still left in SE Ohio, or you drive at least an hour each way to jobs in Columbus or the surrounding area. None of those options sounded good to me, but I had to think of something. I spent hours on this new thing called the World Wide Web, AOL to be specific, that was supposed to help me find an amazing job making lots of money, which would lead to me moving out of my parents' house and moving on with my new life, without basketball. I applied for job after job after job after job, most of which I probably wasn't even interested in and the others I probably wasn't qualified for. I had a degree and played college basketball, what could I NOT be qualified for? I had absolutely no idea how to look for a job and what job to look for, and I can't even remember if I had a resume back then. The only thing resembling "work experience" in my twenty-three years was a three-month summer job at Kroger, five years of playing collegiate basketball, four summers of working basketball camps, and two months of odd temporary jobs from when I was home for the summer of 1996. The only jobs I even got a call back for were the ones that basically said, "If you have a pulse and a car, you can work for us," in other words, sales jobs. And these weren't your glamorous sales jobs like you see in the movies where you get a black American Express card to schmooze with your clients who fly you off to tropical islands for business meetings and you go out to the hottest clubs in the world every night of the week-type sales jobs. No, these were the ones that you walked door to door or you cold-called everyone you have ever met in your life to get them to buy whatever it is they wanted you to sell. Yeah, sounds amazing, right?

My first three years in the real world were anything but amazing. I think I tried my hand at just about any type of temporary position I could; I didn't set my sights too high. I spent the next few years as a temporary quality assistant at a manufacturing plant, two months as a computer product salesperson, two years as a substitute teacher, and, finally, three months as the city pool manager. I didn't mind that the work I was doing had nothing to do with my five years of undergraduate study, I was making money, and I was living with my parents. The only bills I had to pay were my car payment and a few credit card bills I had accumulated in college. The break that my brain was taking during this time was also extremely conducive to drinking and staying out late at least three nights a week. And when I say late, I mean early, early morning. There are plenty of times when I woke up at a friend's house after a few hours' sleep, drove home to grab a quick shower and change my clothes, and then go into work, stale alcohol likely still seeping from my pores. I didn't do anything illegal during this time, but I was not in a good place. I wasn't trying to do anything to get out of my current career situation. I was drinking more and more; many nights I would black out and not remember anything that happened from the night before. I have many stories that I would like to erase from my memory, but sometimes I can look back at those times and realize how far I have come and thank God that I didn't stay in that place very long.

In 2002, I decided to return to the state that I so desperately wanted to leave to start over just three years before. I was interviewed and accepted a job coaching college women's basketball at a small school in Western Massachusetts. Part of me wanted to give coaching a shot, thinking that maybe this is what I was supposed to be doing. Basketball was a huge part of my life; I assumed it was always supposed to be. A bigger part of me wanted to run away from the last two years and leave all of it behind. No one here knew the things I had done, the type of person I had become since graduating from UMASS. I was nervous because I had never been a head coach of a high school team, let alone a college team. Thankfully, the expectations for this team were much lower than my (decreasing) self-esteem at that time. The prior year the team had gone zero something and my successor left after a scandal involving a sexual relationship with one of the players on the team. To their defense, they did end up married with two kids, so it wasn't just a fling, but obviously it was inappropriate and it cost him his job. Trust me, I'm not one to throw stones from my glass castle, but we will get to that later.

I was excited for this new fresh start, hoping I could find the career I was looking for and maybe, just maybe, I could find a meaningful relationship (more). On the first days on campus, I met a few people and went out for drinks with a few of the coaches, things were going pretty well, and I settled right in. Once the students started to arrive on campus, that's when I knew this thing was for real. I was going to find out quickly if I had what it took to be a college basketball coach if I was one of those players who could play the game but had no idea how to teach the game.

Before I would start my coaching job, I first had to fill the role as assistant sports information director and cover the men's soccer team to report the results to the local newspapers and the conference SID. As I was getting ready to leave my office to drive up to the off campus fields, the athletic director stopped by my office and he introduced me to one of the students, a former player on the men's basketball team who was finishing up his degree. He seemed like a nice kid, he was polite, and he was about six foot and nine inches, so I could have guessed that he was somehow associated with the basketball team. I would see him quite a few times over the next few days and weeks as he worked the men's soccer games chasing down soccer balls that had gone out of bounds and away from the field. I also played pickup games with the men's team and some former players; obviously, this was when I could still walk and run up the court without passing out from exhaustion!

About a month into the school year, one of my players sent me an instant message over AOL saying that there was someone who had been asking about me and if I was dating anyone. I was intrigued, but I had no idea on earth who she would be talking about and it was kind of awkward that it was one of my players who was trying to play matchmaker. Come to find out, that tall, quiet, polite kid (I was only twenty-six, so it's not like I was an old fart!) that I had met in my office and had seen many times around campus was "feeling me." I had to stop and think before I said anything. I had only been on campus for a month and I wasn't sure I was ready to think about anything but coaching at that point, and I certainly didn't think I was ready to start my career with a scandal!

I finally ended up telling her that she could tell him to stop by my office someday if he wanted to. I figured it was just a joke and he wasn't really serious and that I would probably never see him around my office anytime soon; I was kind of trying to call his bluff. A day or two later, guess who showed up in my office? OK, smart ass, now what? We just sat and talked about nothing, including nothing about him being attracted to me or anything along those lines. He stopped by a few more times over the next few days, but again, we just talked about basketball; I told him about this kid named LeBron James from Akron, Ohio, who was going to be the next Jordan (yeah, I called it!). He told me about his basketball career and why he wasn't playing this year. A transfer rule along with some yellow tape and a lack of support from some school officials resulted in a premature end to his collegiate basketball career and a year serving as a student assistant for the men's basketball team while he finished his degree. Finally, one weekend I was driving out toward Boston for a recruiting showcase where girl and boy high school basketball players would be showing their skills in front of small northeast college coaches. So, I asked if he wanted to go with me, to do some "recruiting" for the men's team. He accepted and I really don't remember if I was happy or nervous, but I'm pretty sure I asked myself at least one hundred times what the hell I was doing!

Other than stopping for subs for lunch, I honestly don't remember much about that trip. And it's not because I didn't have a good time; it was because everything was a whirlwind after that. Although I wasn't sure what I was doing when I first asked him to join me, I actually had a good time and I looked forward to seeing him again, whatever that meant. Over the next week or so, we started to hang out (I think that's what the kids were calling it) at my apartment because we certainly couldn't go to his dorm room/campus town-house and risk being seen by my players or any other student on campus, for that matter. We stayed up watching trashy and mindless television shows like *Blind Date*, *Cheaters*, *Fifth Wheel*, *ElimiDate*, etc. until 3:00 or 4:00 a.m. I was exhausted, but I was intrigued. At first, I wasn't sure he seemed like my type; other than basketball, we didn't have that much in common. He was from the city; I was from Southeastern Ohio. He was twenty-two; I was not twenty-two. He had a past that was much more "exciting" than mine in that he wasn't such the goody two-shoes that I was; I think I actually told my mom that he was "thuggish" when I first told her about him. But we clicked. I don't know what it was. There was something that I wanted to learn more about. It was so easy to talk to him. We talked for hours and it wasn't forced. Yeah, based on what I talked about earlier with my first two years out of college, you probably think there was some other reason we stayed up all night, but we really did spend the majority of that first week talking and getting to know each other. OK, we shared a bed. I mean, how could I let him drive a whole one half mile down the road after drinking and staying up until 4:00 a.m.? That would have been rude. The first time we kissed was probably more uncomfortable and awkward than my first kiss in high school, but I knew I wanted to try again.

I remember one night that first week that he didn't come over to hang out and he called while I was sleeping and left a voicemail. I must have listened to that voicemail over a hundred times. There was nothing special about what he had said; he hadn't professed his undy-ing love for me and he also didn't tell me to go kick rocks. He was just really sweet and had taken time out of his busy college-drink-ing-at-4:00 a.m. life to call me, a lonely out of town twenty-six-year-old college basketball coach to tell me that he was thinking of me that he couldn't wait to see me again. Now, he could have totally been blowing weed smoke up my butt and I probably never would have known the difference. But I was just going to let it run its course and let things fall as they may. I mean, really, how long could something last between a twenty-two-year-old student finishing up his final year of college and a twenty-six-year-old college basketball coach who already had her life figured out? Wow, I can't believe I was actually able to type that and pretend like it was true! I would have convinced myself, if I wasn't there to experience it.

Looking back, I was so fortunate to have Pat there to support me and help me keep my sanity. I was not accustomed to losing. Sure we had a few losing streaks when I was in college, but we finished every season with a winning season, above point five hundred. I would go out on a limb to say that we underachieved a few of those seasons, which can make it harder to swallow, but the records do not give those teams the credit we deserved. I'm a horrible loser, not gracious at all. Losing does not build character; it makes you the "not winner."

After 2 excruciating seasons and a record of 6-40, I decided I had had enough. I didn't like the snow; I wrecked my car twice in the snow in a one-year span. I didn't like Division III basketball. I had some good kids on the team that I really enjoyed being around, but it just wasn't for me. At this point, I didn't like coaching. I applied for an MBA program back in Columbus at Franklin University, and the minute I was accepted, I was packing my stuff and heading back to Ohio. My dad had always told me after I graduated from UMASS that I should have gotten my master's with my fifth year of eligibility, but I had no interest in being in school for an extra year after completing my senior year of basketball.

I didn't really talk to Pat about my decision; I just applied to see if I would be accepted and then we could have that conversation when it was time. Fortunately, when I did finally talk to him, he didn't even think about it; he wanted to get out of North Adams as quickly as I did. His father had died the previous year and his mother had moved to Florida, so to him, he had nothing to stick around Massachusetts for. I'm not sure if that relieved me or scared me because it added a whole new pressure to the entire situation. If this was another one of my crazy ideas that would end up blowing up in my face, well, now it was going to blow up in my face and someone else's face. I wouldn't be able to move back in with my mom and dad long term because I was bringing someone with me. That meant I was going to have to figure it out, make it work, and be a grown up. That probably scared me the most. I wasn't ready to grow up.

CHAPTER 5

Everything Happens for a Season

In September 2004, we packed up both of our cars and my parents' truck and made the seven hundred-mile trek to Ohio. Pat had "inherited" a 1993 Toyota Camry from his father and I'm honestly surprised it made it out of North Adams, let alone across three states! We must have stopped three or four times so that his car would cool down and he could put oil in it! I usually made that trip in about ten hours. I think it took us closer to thirteen with all of the stopping for oil, food, and bathroom breaks!

Once we got settled in, we both had to find jobs. We ended up applying to be substitute teachers in the Logan-Hocking school district, something we were both already familiar with. Pat started before I did because I was still trying to find a job that I thought was much more in line with my education and background and my bank account was also calling for something a little more lucrative than seventy dollar a day! Pat had landed a more permanent position as a classroom aide for the special education class at the high school. At first, it was a pretty cushy job. He would sit in the class and monitor the kids to make sure they weren't causing too much disruption for the teacher and the rest of the class, and if they did, he would take them out of the classroom. I'm guessing at 6'9" about 250 lbs, they thought he might be a motivating factor for the kids to stay in line. Eventually he was assigned to one particular student who had a history of trouble and he had been through his fair share of aides. For the most part, the kid was okay; he had his moments of outbursts and inappropriate behavior in class, but that was true for all of the students in that room. However, one day, everything changed. He had to take the student into the hallway because he was not able to calm down and sit in the class without causing problems with another student. As they sat outside the room, the kid had a pencil that he was fumbling around with, fidgeting to pass the time. Out of nowhere, he pulls back his arm as if he were a major league pitcher and swings full force at Pat, stabbing him in the shoulder with the pencil! Now, Pat can be intimidating because of his size and he had some temper issues in college, but he had never shown any sort of behavior like that since I had been with him. This kid had no idea what was coming. As quickly as he stabbed, Pat picked him up out of the desk and pinned him against the lockers on the wall. I can't remember exactly what he was yelling at him, but I doubt it is any-thing I would want to repeat in a PG-13-rated book! The kid is lucky that the teacher, the principal, and the resource officer arrived at the scene as swiftly as they did or I'm not sure he would have made it out with all his limbs and appendages attached. Pat came home from school with a tear and pencil stain on his shoulder. After he told me the story and said he was okay, I was mad that the he ripped one of my favorite shirts I had bought for him! Now that kid was lucky I didn't get a hold of him!

Our substitute teaching careers came to a close shortly after, as we decided to move out of my parent's house and head up to Columbus where we had more opportunities to find better jobs.

Later that year, my father finally made the decision to retire for good. He had tried to do it a few years before, but he couldn't sit still, he was getting on my mom's nerves, and frankly they needed the money. My parents always had the best of intentions for their lives and their careers, but they hadn't been lucky with their financial investments over the years. My dad was a blue-collar union man to the bone; Plumbers & Pipefitters Local 189 out of Columbus, Ohio, was his life's work for thirty-five years. He would come home with burns and blisters from chemicals and welding and pitch black hands and fingernails, and he always looked whooped when he got home.

Well, that was after he stopped by the Shamrock to drink a few "soda pops" with a few of the guys he worked with and many that he didn't. I was glad when he was finally able to hang up his welding helmet, as he was about a month shy of his sixtieth birthday and he deserved a break. He had bought a Harley Davidson during his first retirement attempt and he was looking forward to riding all day, every day, and perfecting one of the finest farmer's tan I have ever seen on a man. If there was anyone who deserved a retirement, it was my dad.

Aside from a cold here and there or maybe an occasional bout of the brown bottle flu, my dad never got sick. If he did, I sure didn't know about it. It was rare for him to miss a day of work, and if he did, it was usually because he took the day off to travel to one of my basketball games or track meets. Most men are babies when they have a sniffle, but I'm pretty sure my dad would have still gone to work with a broken finger or leg, and I would not be surprised if he did have a broken finger or two somewhere along the way. He developed a persistent cough that just didn't want to go away; it just kept hanging on and wouldn't break up, so he went to see our family doctor to get checked out. The doctor ordered a chest x-ray; I'm guessing he thought it might be pneumonia or bronchitis or something very treatable, but nagging. The results of the test indicated a shadow of some sort around the middle of his spine, but he couldn't be sure what it was, so he ordered him to see a specialist to determine what it was and what needed to be done.

In January, we celebrated my dad's sixtieth birthday party with some of our closest friends and family. It was a great time because I was home, my dad had been enjoying his time off, and we were doing one of our favorite pastimes, drinking beer! When it was time to blow out the candles on his cake, my dad just couldn't blow them out in a normal way. He was sitting on a chair, and as he exhaled to blow them out, he fell out of his chair, pretending that the effort was more than he could handle! That was my dad. If you didn't know him well, you would think he was very quiet, a man of few words. But when he was around his friends with a few Bud Light, he was the life of the party. I honestly had more fun hanging out with my parents when I was drinking than most of my friends. There were always good times to be had, many laughs, some minor mishaps, but no drama. It was a fitting celebration for the man that everyone loved and respected and called the reverend (Rev).

Later that week, we received some news from the doctor; the shadow on my dad's spine was a tumor. What we thought was a feisty cold or maybe walking pneumonia ended up becoming something even more uncertain. We had to go to a specialist to see what the next steps were, but I'm not sure that we ever really prepared for what the outcome or cause could be.

I never knew my dad to be afraid of anything. He used to race dirt bikes when he was younger. I once saw him knock down a nest of yellow jackets from a tree in our yard and then run back to the house with a swarm of bees stinging him from head to toe. I know that he didn't like to go to the doctor, but who really likes to go to the doctor? But I saw a look in his eye that I had never seen before as she told him that he would need to have surgery to remove the tumor and have it evaluated to see if it was malignant. Malignant, that meant cancer. I'm not sure if my dad was more upset by the actual process of going into the hospital to be cut open by someone he'd met just one time or if he was afraid of the results. I'm not sure if I was more upset at seeing my dad, hugging my mom and crying like a helpless child, something I had never seen before or at the word malignant. That wouldn't be the last M word that I would come to hate in the coming weeks.

About a week later, my dad entered the hospital to have the tumor removed and tested. The surgery itself was to be pretty straightforward: go in, grab the tumor, and come back out. Well, because of the size of the tumor, it ended up being about the size of an egg, and the fact that it was just a bloody mess, he needed to have a blood transfusion to replace what he had lost during the extraction process. But for the most part the initial surgery went well (we will talk about that "initial" part later); we were just anxiously awaiting for the results of the biopsy to see where that egg-shaped monstrosity had come from.

I was working a temporary contract job on the upper side of Columbus at the time, and it was the most boring job I have ever had in my life. I sat at a front desk taking calls from construction workers on job sites who were having issues with the computer system that our company made. Sounds fun, right? Well, I did have at least one or two calls a day that would provide me some comic relief, as you can imagine with mostly middle-aged, southern men who had worked in concrete their whole lives. Having a computer system to tell them how to do their job was probably something they were still wrapping their heads around and I tried to be as sweet and patient as I could possibly be. I won't get into too much detail about the calls, but essentially there was this thing called a junction box that housed all of the brains of the computer and that is also where their machine number was; that was the number they needed to give me so that I could patch them to a technician. Around the office, it was more affectionately known as a J box, genius. Well, you would have thought I asked for the national security code to a nuclear bomb. Most calls went something like this, "Sir, I need your machine number. Do you have that?" "Machine number, what's that? You mean my phone number?" "No, sir, please look in your J box and tell me the five-digit number you see there." "J box? What in the hell is a J box?" "Sir, it's the junction box, probably to your left if you are standing next to it right now." "Well, I'm standing here and I sure don't see no box and it sure as hell don't say J box." The best part about this whole process was, even after spending too many minutes of my life, I can never get back explaining to this man what a J box is and where to find it (and sometimes I wanted to tell them where to put it); I then had to place them in a queue for the next available technician to pick up and call them back. I can't tell you how many new swear words and combinations of swear words I learned in that six-month position.

On February 13, I got the call that would change the course of my family's life forever. My mom called me on my cell phone to tell me, "Your dad has cancer." Not only did he have cancer, but it was stage four, which meant that it had spread from one part of his body to another; it had metastasized. They determined that he had renal cell carcinoma, better known as kidney cancer, and he may have three to six months to live. I don't remember much after that. I just remember telling my manager that I had to go and the next thing I know I'm in the hospital running up to my dad's room in a fog. I'm not even sure how I got to the hospital. I'm pretty sure I drove about 90 mph, and if I got pulled over, well, he would just have to follow me to the hospital and give me the ticket in the elevator. Nothing was keeping me from my mom and dad. Besides, this was the reason I was brought back to Ohio; I was now learning.

When I realized that I would have another year of athletic eligibility after my never-ending knee injuries, my dad told me then that I should get my MBA instead of taking on a double major. I was just ready to get done with classes and move on with my life, so I ended up with a BS and BA. My dad did say that he was sure that I got the correct degree because of the initials. Some might take that as a backhanded slap in the face, but if you know anything about my dad, you know he was the king of BS and this was the highest compliment he could give me! So, I guess it shouldn't seem so beautifully ironic to me that the very same day my dad was diagnosed with cancer, I was to begin my first class in the MBA program at Franklin University, seven years after I graduated from UMASS. Much to his displeasure, I put off earning my MBA one more time as I called to move my start date to the next cohort beginning in June.

Chapter 6

Snow, Ice, and Diamonds

Later in 2005, Pat and I decided to take the plunge and buy a house together. You will learn that we did everything completely backward compared to what most couples do, not sure if that was good or bad. I'm not sure when we started talking about a house or even why, but I would venture a guess that a good portion of it was out of fear because of what we were going through with my dad. I say "we" because Pat and my dad had become very close in the three years we were together, even more so after we moved to Ohio. They were so much alike that it sometimes left me thinking that Pat was my dad's long-lost son!

I needed my dad to know I was being taken care of. I wanted him to know that someone he trusted loved me so that if the doctor's original three-to-six months prediction came true, he could die knowing his little girl would be okay. I was the one telling everyone else that doctors are not fortune tellers and that God is the only one who knows when it's our time to make the walk through the pearly gates. But most days, I was trying to convince myself that he was going to live. Every time I went to bed, I feared that I would wake up to a call or text from my mom that the cancer had won and had taken him away from us. I had so many things to do with my dad; I never thought in a million years that I would be thinking about losing the first man I ever loved. I thought he would live forever. Some people feel like they should make up for lost time after they have lost someone in their lives and they later reunite. I was trying to make up for time that hadn't even happen yet because I didn't want him to miss anything, just in case.

Over the next few years after the cancer diagnosis, our lives were up and down. My mom and dad spent countless hours in and out of doctor's offices and put hundreds of miles on the car driving to treatments in Columbus. I learned throughout the entire ordeal just how strong my mom was. I never doubted her ability to handle tough situations, because I watched her keep our family together after my grandmother died, but I also never acknowledged it. When my grandfather died, he left behind a wife and seven children, my mother being the oldest. When my grandmother had to take on two or three jobs to keep the roof over their heads and food on the table, my mom stepped in to be a second mother to her brothers and sisters. She is still like this today. I doubt she even knows just how much I learned by watching her because it wasn't until I saw her putting herself aside to take care of my dad that I saw what being a wife means. She took her vows very seriously. "Until death do us part" wasn't just a five-word statement that she uttered to the Justice of the Peace in Kentucky when she and my dad married. She meant every word of it and she lived every word of it even more in these difficult days. I know she was tired, sad, mad, and frustrated, but she never let it show. She held all of us up on the days she probably wanted to crash. I can never thank her enough for taking care of my dad, even if she thinks she was just doing her job.

After a few treatments and some very difficult meetings with the oncologist, I think we all had enough with the negative Nancy approach of this doctor and we started to look for other solutions. The surgery to remove the tumor had left my dad's spine understandably unstable. Think about a tree being chopped down with an axe. Once you swing away and begin removing chunk after chunk of wood from the same place, the tree starts to wobble and eventually falls over from the lack of support on that side. Well, my dad's spine was doing about the same. He started to lean forward because his back was not supported where the chunks were removed, along with the tumor. Hindsight is twenty-twenty, but wasn't that something that should have been considered before the surgery? And shouldn't it have been something that was discussed after surgery as a possible complication or potential additional surgery to fix his spine? One might think that would have crossed someone's mind in the process. But you know the adage of what assuming does to you and me?

It only took me a few visits to the doctor with my dad to realize that something wasn't right. I didn't like this guy at all. I try to give everyone the benefit of the doubt when I first meet someone, but I also think I'm a pretty good judge of character. The bedside manner, or lack thereof, was aggravating. The negative tones that he spoke in while we were there was infuriating. This guy thought he was God and it's like he was trying to prove himself right every time his predicted timetable would come and go and he would have to take another crack at it. Three to six months came and went. Then it was another three to six months, and then another. My dad doesn't usually say much, but I think I might have heard him refer to this doctor as a "quack" at one point, and we all knew we had to make the switch.

One advantage about living in Columbus is the Ohio State Buckeyes. But there is another team on that campus made up of heroes doing their job every day, but they don't show up on national television every Saturday afternoon. No, they work behind the scenes and they prefer to keep it that way. But when they win, they save lives; they don't score touchdowns. The James Cancer hospital is one of the most prestigious in the country, even the world, and it is right in our backyard. We were diehard Buckeye fans in my family, but little did we know how much bigger fans we would become of the Ohio State University.

In the two years after Pat and I moved to Ohio, we had some major changes in our lives. From the actual move to finding jobs in a brief time and buying a house, then finding out my dad had cancer, we probably endured more than most do in four years of a relationship. Have you ever seen those short stress quizzes with twenty life events and you check off the ones that happen to you in a span of one to two years? Well, I would guess from a test like that our stress levels would have been on the high end, and we were just about to take it up a notch.

We had been dating for almost five years, and I will admit, I was starting to get a little anxious. I was about ten years old before my dad and mom got married, so living with Pat for five years really wasn't a big deal. But knowing that my dad's health wasn't guaranteed, as nothing in this life ever is, I was terrified that he would not be there to walk me down the aisle and give me over to the man that would assume the responsibilities of taking care of me. I knew how much my dad loved Pat and Pat felt the same about him. But we were going to need to make it official to check one thing off the list that my dad wouldn't have to worry about when he left this world. I didn't want him to worry about me. So, like most woman who hit their peak of patience with a man, I started to drop subtle hints. "I don't see a ring on my finger" was my go-to response when I thought I needed to make it clear that I wanted to get married. Subtle, right? I mean, we had the house, what were we waiting for?

Valentine's Day 2007, we had an awful snow and ice storm in Columbus, Ohio. We woke up that morning and looked outside and all you could see was white. I'm not even sure why we both thought it was a good idea to go to work, because I think half of the city was shut down. We both worked some crazy hours in those early days and we had gotten up at 3:30 a.m., before any cancelations and closings had been announced. As I started to get in my car to drive to work, Pat was having trouble getting in his car because the doors were frozen shut. I stopped and told him to get in and I would drive him to work before I headed to work myself; he worked downtown and I worked near the airport. It wasn't ideal, but we both weren't ones to miss work because, frankly, we needed the money and didn't want to short our hours!

I think it took me about three hours to get him downtown and myself to the airport and then another one hour or so after work to pick him up and head home. The entire city was at a standstill and only fools on a budget would be out in treacherous weather conditions where the freeways were like a ghost town. Oh well, we were hustlers and no snow was going to stop us; we did what we had to do.

When we got home, Pat told me that he was taking my car because he had forgotten to get me a Valentine's gift. Seriously? Did you just see the roads and the lack of drivers on them? There was no way in the world that any store was even open, so I expected him to come home with a bag of chips and six packs of beer, because he wouldn't make it far. The last thing I told him was to make sure he didn't come home with stuffed animals because I didn't want him to go out in the snow and come back with something that silly; I didn't want him to go out at all.

When he came home, he sat down on the couch with a bag and a silly look on his face and handed me the first present, a new CD by Robin Thicke that I had really wanted. Okay, well, it wasn't a stuffed animal, so at least he listened. But then, out comes two little dogs, one gray and one white, holding a red box with a bow. Dude, did you really buy me that and did you do it to be funny or to make me mad? I looked at it and laughed and sat in on the coffee table, as I proceeded to open my new CD. He said, "Well, aren't you going to look inside the box?" Huh? Apparently, the box the dogs were holding was functional; at least the dogs had some sort of purpose after all. I figured it would be some new earrings or a bracelet or knowing him, it could have been a condom! But, no. It was a diamond ring. A diamond ring? If you know anything about the two of us, the next few seconds make sense to you. He said, "Well, do you wanna?" I hugged him and then I think I said yes, but I can't remember one hundred percent! Hey, we did good for not being the romantic types and I wouldn't have our story any other way.

After I called my mom and dad to tell them the good news, I was immediately on the phone to get the date reserved for the location later that year. Our official "dating anniversary" (I swear I never thought I would be THAT girl!) was October 13, and that year that date just happened to fall on a Saturday. Knowing how guys are at remembering dates, I thought it would make it easier on him to remember if we just got married on the same date. I'm always thinking of others, right? Unfortunately the date wasn't available, so we opted for October 6, the weekend before. I had also always wanted an outdoor wedding and getting married in the heat of the summer would not have been an option for my 6' 9"-soon-to-be husband, so October felt "safe." Well, you will see later that nothing was "safe" about that October day!

My dad wasn't much to show his emotions, but I think he was happy when I told them we were engaged. I think he was probably thinking more like, "it's about time," but I do think he was also relieved, to some extent. This was all about two years after his cancer diagnosis and we knew it could take him from us at any point with no notice at all. He had been fairly stable, but that didn't keep the thought of him not being there to walk me down the aisle from coming into my mind and maybe his, too. He was already so close to Pat, and they had bonded so much more than I ever imagined; this would just make it official. Little did we know that something else would come up to make us rethink our wedding date.

CHAPTER 7

Cupid's Arrow

June 13 is my parent's "official" wedding anniversary, the date they finally got married when I was ten years old. It is also the day they found out that they were going to be grandparents. I told you we did everything out of order in this relationship, so of course I would get knocked up five months before my wedding! I had gone to work that day and just hadn't been feeling right. Aunt Flow was about a week or two late and she always showed up on time so I figured I was just stressed about the wedding and the new job I had started in April. I stopped at the store on the way home from work and grabbed an EPT and figured I wouldn't tell Pat, because there probably wasn't anything to tell. Well, that's what I get for thinking. I took test number one, and when the double blue line showed up, I had to look at the box about a hundred times to make sure I had it right. So, I took test number two, and shockingly it came back with the same result. If I had one hundred more tests, I would have taken it one hundred more times and I still wouldn't have been convinced that I was about to become a mother. I went downstairs to tell Pat, and I can still see the look on his face. He always claimed to have "super sperm," and his first words were actually, "I knew it!" He said he knew the minute that he, ahem, well, you know what he did, he knew it was the one. He knew he was making a baby that night. I don't know if guys actually have that sense and why on earth they think they have some supernatural ability to know when their little swimmers are going to

51

turn into a bigger swimmer, but he seemed proud of himself, so I let him have his moment!

I'm not sure why, but when my mom answered the phone and I went to tell her, I burst into tears! I don't know if it was the hormones already wreaking havoc on my emotions, with the fact that I would now have to take out the wedding dress that I had just taken IN or that I had no idea how in the world I was going to be a mother! If I was a betting woman, I would say it was all of the above with a little excitement that my dad was going to get a chance to meet his grandchild, just a few months after he would gain a son-in-law. I didn't get to see my dad's face when he found out, but I knew that he and my mom were over the moon to be grandparents, no matter how cool they tried to act. Things were going well for our family and we had good things to look forward to instead of doctor appointments and surgeries and scans, what had become our lives for the previous two years.

One of my favorite stories about my dad is one that my mom told me when I was in college. I'm not sure what brought up the conversation, but my parents were talking about me and what I had accomplished, something along those lines. My parents were very proud of me, so of course they were talking about me! Anyway, my dad had always wanted a boy when my mom was pregnant, what dad doesn't want a boy? But my dad told my mom, "I think I got the best of both worlds" when she asked him if he still wished I had been a boy. To some people, that might sound a little weird, not exactly what you would want to hear someone say about you. But I know what he meant and it might be one of the best things my dad has ever said about me. Despite that, I knew that adding Pat and now a baby boy (there, I gave it away!) to our family would make him a very happy man and give him another reason to live and fight against cancer.

I would say that I had a fairly easy pregnancy. Very little morning sickness, only gagging when I brushed my teeth, heartburn like my esophagus was set on fire and I was drinking gasoline, and I craved French fries. I always craved French fries, so I think I just used pregnancy as an excuse to eat them whenever I wanted and to send everyone around me on a trip to find fries because I was "eating for two." Other than that, I didn't know what the big deal was with pregnancy. Also, being almost six-feet tall, I didn't grow out, he just grew up, and I didn't have much more than a beer belly, well, without the beer, of course. I actually loved being pregnant. It was an amazing feeling when he rolled and kicked and hiccupped, even when he shoved his elbow or knee up into my ribs at the most inopportune time in a work meeting. I was able to connect with him and learn about him way before anyone else would even get to meet him. I already loved everything about him and I was scared to death that something would happen to him and he would either come out with some sort of disorder or he wouldn't make it at all. I'm sure every mother goes through that, questioning their ability to carry a child for nine months while keeping themselves healthy.

If I had the world's easiest pregnancy, my husband had the world's easiest delivery experience. There was no call because my water broke. There were no trips to the hospital for false labor. Nope, he got none of that fun. I showed up at the hospital for an induction at 7:00 p.m. and I had an entire week to pack and prepare for it. My mom decided she would be at the hospital with me to welcome her first grandchild, so she made sure my dad was all comfortable at home and made arrangements for him to ride to the hospital with one of my aunts the next morning. It just so happened that the night I was being induced was also the night of the annual Duke-North Carolina rivalry game, although I really shouldn't be surprised at that at all! While my mom and husband laid on the not-so-comfy fold-out beds in the delivery room, I was laying in the not-so-comfy hospital bed trying to breathe through the pain of labor. Every so often, a good one would hit me, and I would let out a huge exhale while they both just stopped and looked at me like I was the angry wolf huffing and puffing to blow down the little piggy's house. Actually, I felt more like someone had just stabbed me in the stomach and the next person that came near me was going to get a swift kick in whatever area was closest to my foot at that point. It's probably best that they just laid there and looked at me!

Labor started not long after I was injected with Pitocin and around 4 a.m. I had finally dilated enough to get the delightful, life-changing epidural that everyone had told me about. Despite the many surgeries I have been through in my life, I still cannot stand needles. I'm the person that they tell to look away when they are about to stick a needle in your body and instead I stare right at the spot, as if I could will away the pain and the sting with just my menacing, pitiful stare. It's never worked. This would, however, be the first shot I had ever taken in my spine. I've been stuck in my hind quarters, my mouth, my arm, and even my knee—that needle was HUGE!—but I wouldn't be able to watch when they stuck this one in my back. My husband is even more squeamish than I am when it comes to these things and he may even have a worse poker face than I do. I'm looking at him to keep my calm while they are prepping me and all I see is him making this God awful, scrunched up face like he has just eaten the most disgusting thing ever. Thanks for the support, honey.

At about 9:00 a.m. or so, my mom and my husband decided they had worked up an appetite with all the excitement of the last few hours, so they went to get some breakfast. If you have ever been pregnant and been at the hospital to deliver, you know all about the ten different nurses who come in every single hour to poke and prod you in places that you didn't even knew existed. I'm pretty sure everyone in the entire hospital saw my lady parts that day, and there was nothing I could do about it but lay there and smile and say thank you. "Thank you for looking at my lady parts, kind stranger. Come back and visit anytime."

Unfortunately, after all that time, I had still only dilated to 4 cm and it wasn't favorable that I would get much further than that any time soon. I had been lying mostly on my back the entire night, so I tried to lie on my side to see if we could get the party started and get him moving around and ready to make his guest appearance. I guess I can tell you at this point since you already know it's a boy, as did we, his name is Tyson. We were waiting for Tyson Granville Michael Reardon to make his debut. It took us some time to get to the final agreed-upon name. We went everywhere from Seamus to Jalen and then landed on Tyson, and it just stuck from there. Granville was my husband's dad's middle name; he passed away of a heart attack in 2003, just after we started dating. Michael is my father's name; I was adamant that his name had to be in there. My dad's middle name was Eugene, and there was no way my dad would let my child be named Eugene; he didn't even like it himself! Tyson Granville Michael Reardon, this kid was going to love us when he started learning how to write his name in kindergarten!

As I rolled over to my right side, the nurses noticed that Tyson's heart rate was going down, so I had to either stay on my back or roll to my left. At this point, I was so incredibly uncomfortable and antsy and ready to get this kid out of me, but he wanted no part of that. This is when I realized this kid was going to be special, maybe a little spoiled, and he was going to do things his way and in his own time. I could already tell that there was something about him in the way he moved during my pregnancy. All day long, he never stopped moving. He made me tired just in the way he flipped and flopped. If I didn't already know it, I would have sworn I was having twins or maybe even triplets. Lord, help me if I would have had triplets!

At about 10:00 a.m., the nurses came in to tell me that they were calling my OB-GYN and we were going to do a C-section. All I could do was cry. I'm not even sure if they got the entire sentence out before I started sobbing. I don't know if I was sad or mad or disappointed that I wouldn't be able to have a "normal" delivery, or if it was just something I hadn't planned for. I always tried to plan everything in my life, and if it didn't go as planned, well, that was unacceptable and sent me into a tailspin. Besides that, my husband and mom were still down in the cafeteria apparently having a five-course breakfast while I was up in the room about to have a nervous breakdown! Okay, I may be a little dramatic, but this is the way I remember the story and no one is here to tell you otherwise!

I called on my cell phone and told them they needed to get their butts back upstairs because I was about to go back for a C-section. I think they tried to ask me all these questions about what was going on and why, but I think I might have hung up on them! While we waited for them to get to the room and the doctor to arrive at the hospital, the nurses came in to get me prepped, both physically and mentally. This might be too much information, so if you don't like that sort of thing, go ahead and skip a few paragraphs. I have this book on my heart and with it I have to tell it all, even the TMI parts. One nurse comes in with a razor and says that she has to remove the extra "covering" from my lower parts where they are going to give me a trendy bikini line scar, as not to ruin my future swimsuit modeling career. The conversation went kind of like this: "You don't have to do that." "Yes, I do, it's required." "No, you really don't have to do that." "It's okay. I promise it will be quick." (I'm sure that's not the first time a woman has heard that line when talking about her lady region!) Finally she pulled up the sheet and my gown and says, "Oh, I see. I really DON'T need to do that. Wow, the times sure have changed since I was your age!" I'll leave it at that and let you fill in the blanks!

After what felt like an hour, my mom and husband finally made it back from breakfast as I was just getting ready to be wheeled into the operating room. They had given me something in my IV to make me a little more comfortable and a little more out of it, but just before we made it into the room, I heard someone say, "Hey, that's Tez. I know her." Come to find out, one of the nurses in the room would be the sister of a girl I graduated high school with; I had known her and her family for years! I'm sure whatever I said to her was nowhere near audible and probably didn't make much sense, but it was comforting to know that someone I knew would be there to take care of me and Tyson.

Pat had already made the decision nine months prior that he was going to stay north of the border no matter if it was a C-section or a grunt and push birth. What a wuss! I wanted him to be the one laying behind the sheet so that I could be the first person to see my son come into the world! Having been through five prior knee surgeries, I figured the room would be pin-drop quiet and that I would hear the doctor saying, "Scalpel, more light here, where did I put that glove?" What I got was my OB-GYN at one end talking about last night's episode of *American Idol* and who they thought was going to win it all and the anesthesia doctors at my head talking about Bobby Knight getting fired at Texas Tech. Well, I guess everything was going as planned, or they were trying to trick me into thinking that nothing was wrong by being so nonchalant with their operating room banter. I got to lay there and listen to them while watching my husband in his hospital gown and mask turn ghost white, looking as though he was either going to pass out or turn and run straight out of the room at the first site of blood or "baby juices." I started to think that maybe I should have asked my mom to be in the room with me, but then she probably would have been in the conversation about *American Idol* and Tyson would have come out even later than he did!

Finally, at 10:42 a.m. on February 14, 2008, Tyson made his grand, fashionably late appearance. I kissed him on the head. They whisked me off to a cold, lonely recovery room, and he got some poking and prodding of his own. Pat came down to see me after I woke up and told me that the reason he wasn't coming down the birth canal was the umbilical cord was wrapped around his neck. Now, mind you, this was before I had even seen him for more than a kiss in the operating room, so I immediately thought something was wrong with him. But he was healthy, with a good set of lungs, and he was upstairs being cleaned up for his big first date with his mommy. Of course, during my sleeping time, my mom and husband took advantage of the circumstances and had already gotten to see him and hold him and spend time with him. You would think they had planned this all along. I think that's why they had such a long breakfast; they were plotting to steal him away from me!

My dad had stayed home while my mom came to be in the hospital with us, but he was on his way to meet his grandson a few hours later with my aunt and cousin. This was a bittersweet time for our family because almost exactly three years to the day, we were in the same hospital for a much different reason. That is when and where my dad was diagnosed with cancer. From this point on, we didn't celebrate Valentine's Day. No, our day would be spent celebrating Tyson's entrance into our lives and another year of survivorship for my dad.

We were all waiting for my dad to arrive at the hospital; we just couldn't wait to see the look on his face when he met his new little buddy. There had been so many ups and downs and disappointments in the past three years that we all could use a little reprieve, something to give us hope and excitement. It wasn't long and here he comes, bounding through the hospital door; I'm not even sure that he said so much as hi to me, as I laid in the hospital bed. I reiterate that he was actually bounding, and that was something he hadn't been able to do in some time due to the havoc that his back and spine had sustained. He damn near looked like he was floating across the finish line in the one-hundred-meter dash, ready to receive his gold medal. It was another two to three minutes before my aunt and my cousin arrived in the room; he had left them in the dust the minute he climbed out of the car, ran onto the elevator, and high tailed it to my private room!

I still have the very first picture of him holding and staring at Tyson with eyes of adoration I had never seen on my dad. He wasn't one to show emotion, but I don't think there was a dry eye in the room, including the nurses. Here we were, our little family finally complete. We had welcomed into the world the most perfect, beautiful little boy, who was sent to be an angel on earth for our aching souls. I know he was born on Valentine's Day for a reason—because he shot an arrow right through all our hearts that day, our very own real-life cupid.

CHAPTER 8

Walk the Talk

From the moment my dad was diagnosed, I searched for ways to get involved, whether it was directly with his cancer battle or to help ensure that others never had to go through this. The first major leap I took into advocacy was with a local Relay for Life sponsored by the American Cancer Society. My original intention was to volunteer on the planning committee or fundraise as part of a team. I had never been good at asking people for money, even for a good cause, so I was leaning more toward helping the committee recruit people who were way more equipped to beg for money than I was! Besides, I was working a third-shift temporary job which meant I had plenty of time during the day to set up meetings, send emails, or take care of any other administrative items that others might not have the luxury to do. I first met with the regional ACS representative who oversaw organizing the committee and producing any of the event paraphernalia needed. I'd like to say that I was assigned to lead one of the event committees, but I walked away from this discovery session as the chair of event. What in the world did I know about running a fundraising event? Maybe it wouldn't be so bad, because now I wouldn't have to do any groveling; I could tell people they needed to grovel more!

At the end of that first event (you can guess by now that I had caught the volunteer bug), we had raised over twenty thousand dollars, and I had the chance to meet other cancer survivors and their families. That was the first time I had heard the term "survivor" to describe someone who was fighting cancer. Millions of people are living with and battling this vicious beast they call cancer. I hate even giving it the dignity of having a name, but I just assumed they were cancer patients or people living with cancer. It was over time that I realized and truly grasped the meaning and the power of the word survivor. From the minute a person is diagnosed to the second they take their last breath, they are considered a cancer survivor. It doesn't matter how down and out they may look or feel or how long they have fought; each day they wake up a survivor. How awesome is that? And from the survivors I have met since my impolite introduction to cancer in 2005, they are also thrivers. Cancer diagnoses used to be a death sentence. Your family started to plan your funeral and made sure all your estate was together. Hell, they may have even started sneaking the things that they wanted to "remember you by" right from under your nose. Friends would already be talking about you in the past tense, "Oh, Sally was such a lovely lady. It's a shame what the cancer did to her." You would get the sad puppy dog look from everyone you encountered and they would take you by the hand to give you their condolences, but they were never going to hug you because they might get it from you. Okay, that last part might have been a little exaggerated, but you get where I'm going. Cancer research has come a long way; there are more and more people living with and surviving cancer every day. But there are still more and more people living with and surviving cancer every day.

There are plenty of conspiracy theorists in the world that believe cancer was invented by the government to control the population, while also making bajillions of dollars on cancer treatments and medication that no cancer survivor could ever afford in one hundred years. Honestly, I could never give politicians enough credit to believe they could come up with a plan to "invent" a disease that kills millions of people every year. Now, if you told me some sophomore kid at the University of South Whatchamacallit discovered cancer from a science experiment he was conducting in his refrigerator in his dorm room, I might be more inclined to jump in on the theory. Regardless if it was the government, the media, a college dropout, or aliens from the planet Zargon, we have to fix it. We can throw money at it all day long, but unless there is money going to the doctors and researchers who are in the trenches developing the trials and treatments for cancer thrivers, we will be fighting a raging California wildfire with a squirt gun.

In 2009, my employer at the time, NetJets, a private aviation company owned by Warren Buffett catering to celebrities, CEOs, and general folks who have too much money and don't know what to do with it, announced a partnership with the James Cancer Hospital at OSU for a bike ride called Pelotonia to raise money for continued cancer research. This was going to be huge. The James was already one of the best cancer hospitals in the country, as well as the world, and shoveling more money into the system would allow them to bring in the best and brightest doctors from all over the planet to Columbus to do one thing—end cancer. Once I found out that the ride would wind right through my hometown to the campus of Ohio University in Athens, I was in. When I say "in," I meant to volunteer. I hadn't been on a bike since college and that was a mountain bike. The ride lengths were anywhere from 25 miles to 180 miles and even 25 sounded a little daunting at the time. I was out of shape, I had just had a baby a year earlier, and I was recovering from yet another ACL surgery (this time on my good knee). I would volunteer and do anything I could to help and then I would think about riding the following year. That lasted about a week and the next thing I know, I'm signed up for a 50-mile ride and a $1,200 fundraising commitment. Thankfully with NetJets as the founding sponsor, they matched donations for their riders, so I only had to raise six hundred dollars and the company would chip in the rest. The fundraising sounded much easier than riding the bike!

I borrowed my aunt's mountain bike about a week before the ride and I may have ridden it one time, but I just knew twenty-five miles would be fairly easy and after a break the last twenty-five wouldn't be so bad. I even was as bold as to say I was going to ride an additional twenty-five miles and finish my ride in Logan, since the route would go right by my parent's house. There was also a cool factor about this first ride because Lance Armstrong, face of Livestrong, seven-time Tour de France winner and cancer survivor, would be the first rider out of the gate starting on the OSU campus. How many people can say that they rode with a Tour de France winner? Be honest, how many people even know what the Tour de France is?

Ride day went something like this:

5:00 a.m.: Alarm goes off.

5:30 a.m.: Leave the house.

6:00 a.m.: Arrive at ground zero along with 2,500 other bikers.

6:30 a.m.: Stuff your face with bananas, peanut butter, and other goofy stuff that "cyclists" eat when they are riding. I was introduced to stuff like "goo" and "butt butter."

7:00 a.m.: Starting gun fires with Lance Armstrong at the helm and I am nowhere near the front of the line, so no riding with Lance for me.

After what seemed like days, I called my mom from the rest stop around mile twenty-five; it was around 10:30 a.m.

Mom: "Hey there! Where are you?"

Me: "I'm at a rest stop in Groveport, about twenty-five miles in."

Mom: "Good job. Oh, Lance just rode by the house. I barely got a picture because he was going so fast."

Me: "Um, it's 10:30 a.m. and that's like mile seventy-five. I think I might be a little ways behind him. Don't expect to see me for a little while."

Seriously. Dude finished the ride at like 12:00 p.m. It took him five hours to ride one hundred miles, and he was cruising. If it hadn't been for stopping to talk to other riders and volunteers in the first few miles of the ride, he probably would have been done by 10:00 a.m. Now, granted, the hills of France are probably much more treacherous and intimidating than those of Southeastern Ohio, but five hours? There is one particular hill on the route that was just awful. It hurt me to walk up that hill, and yes, I own the fact that I walk hills, don't judge me. I was convinced that there had to have been a truck that picked him up and dropped him off somewhere that no one would see him because I just couldn't fathom someone riding that damn fast. There were those associated with the ride that were quite disappointed that he rode so fast and didn't stop to spend much time with spectators, many of whom were cancer survivors. What I knew that other riders did not is that Lance, a NetJets owner (they are called owners as they own shares of a private jet), had a flight scheduled out of a small airport near Athens that was due to leave at 1:00 p.m. for Colorado. I thought it must have had a three- to four-hour slide time, but nope, he made that flight at 1 p.m. and that was the last we saw of Lance.

Thankfully, the ride was such an overwhelming success that I'm not even sure many people noticed or even cared, for that mat- ter. The first Pelotonia ride for cancer raised over $X million with almost 2,500 riders, over 1,000 riders and the morale and spirits of cancer survivors and caregivers all over the state of Ohio. The most impressive part of the model behind Pelotonia is that one hundred percent of all the funds raised by the riders go to the James. You read that right, one hundred percent. Part of the structure of the sponsor- ship from NetJets was a $2.5 million donation that would fund the administrative and planning costs for the ride, making way for each and every dollar to go straight to cancer research. How could you not want to be involved knowing that you are making a direct impact on something that is saving lives? I couldn't imagine not being involved for years and years to come.

I guess you want to know how my first ride went. Well, let's just say I finished and I didn't make it the extra twenty-five miles to get to Logan. After the ride, others told me that with the mountain bike I was riding, it would have been the equivalent to riding double the mileage that I actually completed. Yeah, that's what I was going for. Why take the easy way out of it when you can ride double in the same amount of time? That's my story and I'm sticking to it!

CHAPTER 9

Eight Hours to Heaven

In October of 2010, my mom had called to tell me that my dad made the decision to cease all treatments. His body had enough; I'm sure his mind had enough, too. He still had a blood thinner that he had to give himself to prevent clotting, but aside from that, he was going to let nature take its course. He hadn't told me yet, but my mom told me so that I would be prepared and could handle it without a breakdown in front of him! It had been a long journey on this cancer highway, but it just didn't feel like we were getting any closer to the destination, at least not to the destination we had been hoping and praying for. The holidays were getting closer and he didn't want to tell me then because he wanted them to be special and not worrisome or stressful. But my mom convinced him that he had to tell me, because although there was no way of knowing how long it would be before the cancer takes over his entire body, it may come quicker than expected. From that moment, I strived to make the holidays the best, most memorable times for all of us, even though the end was undeniably near, barring a complete and utter miracle. My dad needed this. Tyson needed this. We all needed this. We would try our best to make Christmas as normal as possible, not sad, no hints of saying goodbye or providing an early memorial service, just normal, whatever that was.

When my father was in Vietnam, he was baptized by a Buddha. My mother still has a box of slides from the time he spent stationed in Japan as an aircraft mechanic; there is a picture of a much younger, much skinnier version of my dad sitting in what looks like some sort of temple being baptized by a Buddha. I had seen this picture so many times in my childhood when I would sneak into my mom and dad's closet to try on my mom's clothes or shoes and I would sit and stare through the slide viewer at beautiful pictures of Mt. Fuji, Japanese statues, and US Air Force airplanes. I had no idea back then what that picture would actually come to mean to our family, some forty years later.

I had several conversations with my dad after his decision to cease all medical treatment to give his body a rest and prepare for the next stage in his life. One day while riding in the car, he said, "You know, we really need to write a letter to the big wigs at the James. I want to say thank you for all they have done for me." Trying to keep myself from losing it and losing control of the car, I told him, "Yeah, that sounds like a good idea." I knew what he was telling me in his so familiar MEK way; he wanted me to write the letter for him and he would read it and send it off. He wasn't just talking about his oncologist, who I believe until this very day was an angel in disguise. Oh no, he was talking about THE doctor at THE James at THE Ohio State University, Dr. Michael Caligiuri, who served as CEO of the cancer hospital. I had the honor of meeting Dr. C a few times at a fireside chat that he hosts regularly on campus for cancer caregivers and survivors, and I also had the chance to ride alongside him in Pelotonia. Well, I wouldn't say alongside him as much as he passed me a few times as I was huffing and puffing at 10 mph and he was gliding along smoothly at 15 mph, talking and shaking hands all the way. That athletic ability I told you about sure did nothing to help my cycling game, but that was never what it was about.

A few weeks before, my mom had made the decision to call in hospice to help manage my dad's pain and to keep an eye on him since he would not be going to his regularly scheduled checkups at the James. He had started to go downhill after Christmas with a great deal of pain along with no appetite and he was starting to hallucinate. I had been spending every weekend with them after Christmas so that I could be there to help my mom in case she needed to do anything, but I knew I also needed to spend as much time with him as I could. I just didn't know how much time I had left.

On one of our trips to visit, my dad started talking about a car being parked in the backyard. My mom had told me before that he was starting to see things and talk crazy about dreams he was having, but I hadn't witnessed it for myself. We were sitting in the living room and my dad was sitting in his computer chair, the same place he had normally been sitting when he was on the computer, usually emailing a group of guys who were in the same unit he had been in during Vietnam. He looked out the back door and asked us if we saw the fender of a car behind the house. Not knowing what was going on, I looked and said, "No, dad, I don't think there is a car in the backyard. Are you seeing a brick or something that looks like a car?"

"No, there is a car in the yard. Can't you see it?" Pat got up and looked outside and had no idea what to say, and I think we actually started to laugh a little. My mom made a gesture to us which was almost like, *Shut up and go with it. This is what I was telling you about!* I could tell that my dad was starting to get a little upset because we didn't see it, so we finally acted as though we actually did see it and then promptly changed the subject! That's when I knew we were starting to lose him. The only time I had ever seen him even remotely this discombobulated was when he had had a few too many adult beverages. He obviously hadn't had anything to drink, however his mind was now constantly in and out of drunkenness, and this time it wasn't funny.

I don't think my dad was ready to die, but he wasn't afraid of it, either. I do think he was ready to be pain-free, mentally and physically. He had suffered so many different ailments and setbacks throughout the entire six-year battle; I still don't know how he did it. My parent's kitchen looked like a pharmacy or a drug dealer's cook house, because of all of the prescriptions and over-the-counter medications. Nothing they tried would take his pain away for more than a quick, momentary release and then it was back, sometimes stronger than it was before. He couldn't sleep; I think my mom told me at some point he didn't sleep for several days. The pain was unbearable and I know how hard it is for me to turn off my brain when I go to bed; I'm sure he had plenty of crazy thoughts in his confused, suffering, frail mind. One night, he told my mom that he thinks the reason he hadn't died yet was because he was baptized by that Buddha in Japan and he didn't think God would recognize that. He needed to make it right with the Lord before he thought he would start to feel some relief, some closure, and some peace.

On January 8, 2011, the day before my thirty-fifth birthday, we were baptized as a family, myself, my mother, my father, and Tyson, by the hospice chaplain. While I had been to church many times with my grandmother and my great aunt Thelma, I had never given my life to Christ. And to be honest, I was only doing it this time because my mom and dad asked me to and I was going to do anything they asked of me. It was a very quick and quiet occasion held right in my parent's living room. We were all pretty emotional as we said the prayers and I really could almost see a huge weight lifted from my father's shoulders. Although his physical condition never changed, perhaps it had even continued to get worse, he did seem to have released some of his worries and anxiety that had consumed him over the previous few months.

Now, if you are reading this book hoping to hear a miraculous story about how my dad was saved from the vise grip of the grim reaper at the very last second and we lived happily ever after, well, I will apologize now. That just isn't going to happen. Sure, he is living happily ever after in heaven riding his Harley Davidson, drinking Bud Light, and catching up with friends and family. But the miracle we had hoped for wasn't meant to be. Notice I didn't say there was no miracle, just not the one we wanted.

The next few pages were hard to write, and I'm sure they will be hard to read, but it's a crucial part of my story, one that I am obligated to tell.

One week after our mini baptism ceremony, I had made plans to go to a girls' basketball game in Logan with a high school friend to watch her niece play. I also had plans to talk to my dad, as my mom had a meeting to go to, and she told me earlier in the week that he was struggling with letting go. She thought that one of the reasons that he couldn't sleep, while being exhausted and filled with pain and frustration, was that he didn't want to leave us. My dad probably worried as much about us as we worried about him during his cancer fight. I know that he was feeling guilty about not taking care of his finances over the years and ashamed that he would leave my mom with no life insurance to cover the bills when he was gone. It bothered him a lot. I also know that he wanted to make sure that my family was going to be okay, that his best buddy Tyson would be okay. I hated that he would not get to see his grandson grow up, because he waited so long for that little joy in his life, and I believe that he lived as long as he did so that he could meet him, even if just for a little while. I also know that he didn't want any of us to see him suffer. He was a proud man and he would not have wanted to be on life support and confined to a nursing home or to a wheelchair. He still wanted to do things on his own and there were times we just had to let him. This day, I had to tell him that it was okay to go, even if it meant that I had to let go, too.

My mom went to her meeting, leaving me alone with my dad and Tyson. He was sitting on the couch, drifting in and out of sleep, in and out of consciousness, while I watched him, waiting for the right time to talk. He looked at me in one of his moments of lucidity and said, "So, PINK is doing okay?" I knew that he was concerned when I left NetJets to enter the world of retail, so I wasn't surprised that he would ask that question. What I didn't know is that it would be the last words my father would ever say to me.

Shortly after that, he got up to go to the bathroom. He was still having trouble keeping anything down, even water, and I knew he was throwing up. I never got to have that talk with him, as he laid down after the vomiting subsided. I went to the basketball game later that night, assuming I would just talk to him the following day. My mom hadn't known that I was planning to spend the night, but as I say, "Everything happens for a reason" and I will be forever grateful that I stayed that night.

When I got home from the game, Tyson was still up being just as wild and silly as ever. He was almost three at the time, his birthday about a month away. I went to put him to bed and my mom asked me to come help her when I was done because my dad had thrown up on himself in bed and she wanted to change his shirt. Neither of us knew what the rest of the night would entail. He kept trying to get out of bed as we cleaned him up, but he wasn't talking. He would moan and move to the end of the bed while my mom told him to lay back down and we would get anything he needed. His eyes were wide open, but he wasn't there. I can't even say for certain if he knew we were there. My mom called the hospice nurse to see if there was anything we could give him to help him sleep or at least make him comfortable. He was restless, and we were catching our breath for what was to come. My mom said later that she knew what was happening because she was there the day my great-aunt Thelma passed away from colon cancer. When she died, she told everyone it was in the water. My parents drank bottled water ever since.

The hospice nurse arrived and took my dad's vitals and then told us he would probably be gone in about eight hours. My life with my dad was coming down to eight hours. I knew this day would come, but I always expected I would get a phone call or text; I never thought I would be in the room when it happened. I'm not sure which way I preferred, but at this point it didn't matter; someone else made that decision for me. That was around 11:00 p.m., and I called Pat to tell him that he should come and say goodbye to my dad; he had stayed home while Tyson and I were in Logan. It hurt me as much to tell him knowing how much my dad meant to him. They got along so well right from the start, Pat just fit right into our family, and my dad knew that I had found someone who would take good care of me. I don't even think he said anymore in that short conversation than, "Okay," and I wasn't even sure if he would even come after I hung up the phone.

My mom gave me some time and told me to go in the room and tell him goodbye and that I love him. My dad and I never had an affectionate relationship and we didn't get too mushy when we talked, even if we were trying to be somewhat serious. Now I had to tell the first man that I had ever loved that it was time for him to leave me and the other man in my life would take over where he left off. I told him I loved him and that he needed to rest and close his eyes. I know he couldn't say anything back to me, but I believe that he heard me. That was our way, we didn't have to talk, and I then realized that our conversation that was supposed to happen earlier that day happened exactly how it should have. It didn't. But he knew what I was there to say. I know that he knew.

CHAPTER 10

Talking to Angels

If you ever hear someone say that so and so, "Died peacefully sur-rounded by friends and family," don't you dare believe it. I am not here to sugarcoat anything and there was certainly nothing sugary or sweet about what transpired that night. While I was so glad to be there to say goodbye to my dad and comfort my mother through his transition, I would be lying if I said it was peaceful. It is one of the most unnerving things I have ever gone through, but I wouldn't change it for the world. To literally watch the life leave the body of someone you love is tragic and almost otherworldly because you can see that they are not there. The mind is gone, but the spirit hangs on as long as it can. I watched as he seemed to fight crossing over, like he was wrestling with a ghost that he didn't want to go with. I don't know if he was scared or confused or relieved. This wasn't like in the movies where you see a patient lying comfortably in bed holding the hand of someone they love saying their final goodbyes. In the mov-ies, they close their eyes and take their final breath and then it's over. Trust me, that ain't how it works. It took every bit of the eight hours the hospice nurse said it would take. It felt like eight days.

After I had my time with him, my mom and I sat together in the room next to his bed and just watched him. She said, "He didn't want you to see him like this." I know he didn't, but I'm glad I was there. I don't think I ever would have been able to live with myself if I hadn't been there. We found a CD player and listened to Dave

Matthew's band *Stand Up* album on repeat all night long to try to get him to relax. It was just as much for us as it was for him. I can't even remember what else we talked about as we sat there awaiting the inevitable; the words are a blur. But I can still remember the smell. I can still hear the music play as we sat there completely defenseless. Pat finally arrived and I took him to the room to see him one last time. He didn't want to go; he was never good with things like that. But, like me, I knew it was something he had to do or he would regret it. There is just something about being there when you know that this is the last time you will see a person alive. We don't get those kinds of chances every day; you just have to embrace it and realize how fortunate you are to be able to say farewell one last time, whether you want to or not.

As the night went on, the house was completely quiet with Tyson asleep in the next room, Pat asleep on the couch, and Dave singing the final soundtrack for my dad. Our entire little family was together in one place for the send-off; I couldn't have choreographed a more perfect ending if I tried. I left my mom in the chair for a few hours to go take a nap, unsure of how much longer we would be waiting. I wanted to give her time to say what she needed to say to the man she had given her life to for almost thirty-seven years. They weren't always easy and I know they had their struggles, but I will always admire them for sticking it out and making it work. It's become so commonplace for people to get divorced because they fell out of love or they got sick of one another. My parents may not have had the perfect marriage, but to me they were perfect for each other. I realized that even more over the six years that my dad was sick. To watch my mother unselfishly give up her freedoms and sometimes her sanity to take care of him was unlike anything I had ever witnessed: unconditional love. "'Til death do us part." That is what she promised and that is what she did. When I told her thank you for taking care of him, she looked at me like I was crazy. "Well what else am I supposed to do? That's my job." She didn't take any credit for anything and she very rarely complained about having to drive him three days a week to Columbus, for his treatments, or staying up all night to take care of him because he couldn't sleep. They were one soul, one person, and she took that very seriously. Not everyone would do that, as much as we would like to believe they would. I looked at my mom in a whole other way after watching how she managed to take care of herself as she took care of him. She is my hero, and I hope that one day, I can be half the wife that she was for my dad.

At around 6:45 a.m., I felt something brush my shoulder; it was my mom. "Tez, he just passed." I thought I was dreaming; this couldn't possibly be happening. I opened my eyes and tried to focus and I could see that this was not a dream. He was gone. Tyson was still sleeping soundly at the edge of the bed, perfectly oblivious to everything that had gone on that night. I was glad that he didn't wake up and come into the room because I'm not even sure I would have known what to say or do. I walked into the room to give him one final kiss on his forehead and to hug my mom, who felt so small and so weak in my arms. But I could feel the relief in her body. She fought just as hard as he did for six long years and now it was over, over.

I asked my mom what happened, and she said she had drifted off to sleep for a few minutes, and when she woke up, he was gone. All I could think was that it was just like him to make sure we were all asleep and comfortable before he decided it was time to do the same.

I walked out in the family room at the back of the house, and Pat was already sitting on the edge of the couch, staring blankly across the room in the dark. I didn't know what to say because I knew he was hurting just as badly as I was. I just sat on the couch with him and cried. There were no words that needed to be said, he was gone, and he took a little piece of all of us with him.

One of the more touching and confusing moments in the entire evening was Tyson's reaction when he finally woke from his naïve, peaceful slumber. My aunts and uncles had arrived at my mom's house to say goodbye before the funeral director came to pick up my dad and prepare him for cremation. Tyson crawled out of bed, as my mom and I tried to get him to go in and give Papaw a hug, and that boy, who always used to run in my dad's room and jump on the bed to greet him, would not go any further than the doorway. It's like there was some sort of force field protecting the doorway and he just bounced right off and quickly ran away from the room. I have always heard that younger children experience the death of a loved one very differently than adults; some believe they can see and talk to the dead. I wouldn't have believed it if I didn't see it with my own eyes. He knew there was something in that room and he didn't go in it that entire day.

On the evening of January 15, 2012, Tyson and I had gone to bed. It was extremely difficult for him to fall and stay asleep on his own, more on that later, but I would lay in bed with him until he fell asleep. At about 11:00 p.m., I woke up to the bed bouncing, thinking Tyson had to go to the bathroom or he couldn't sleep. It was neither. He wasn't saying a word, but it was like he was playing with an imaginary friend. He would jump and romp and play with his hands, but he never made a sound, never opened his eyes. This went on until about 6:45 a.m. the next morning, January 16, one year to the day, to the hour of my dad's death. He laid down and fell asleep, although I don't think he was ever awake throughout the entire night, at the very moment my dad would have taken his final breath one year before. Tyson finally had his chance to say goodbye to his Papaw with this midnight rendezvous play session. I have never witnessed something so supernatural and inexplicable, and I wondered if I had dreamed the entire thing up. I was also somewhat jealous that he got to see him one more time.

CHAPTER 11

One Million Ways

Months before I lost my father to cancer, I started a new job at a well-known local fashion retailer in Columbus, Ohio. I'll protect the innocent by saying, "It's a secret." I had worked in aviation for about five years and had made some tremendous strides in my career, but I needed more. I knew I was underpaid for the work I was doing compared to my co-workers and that never sat right with me. I was ready to try something new and, frankly, make more money. I would say my dad was a little disappointed when I left the aviation job because he was in the Air Force, and it was something we could talk about and he would be able to relate. What in the world would we talk about with this new "secret" job other than he wore the same type of garments they sell, just not as pretty? I think he was also slightly concerned that I was making a risky move by leaving a company where I had already established myself as a hard worker and that the grass (or money) might not be greener on the other side.

I had already ridden in Pelotonia for two years with NetJets (don't worry, I finally bought a real fancy road bike like the other "cyclists"), and the company I was now going to work for had a team that supported the ride. I wouldn't go as far as to say I left NetJets because of the disappointing way the company reneged on their partnership with Pelotonia, but I would be lying if I said it didn't play at least a small part. One of the first questions I asked when I arrived

75

for my first week was, "Who is in charge of your Pelotonia team and how can I help."

Even before my dad died, I had talked to several people about making the Pelotonia team bigger and better and I wanted to help drive the involvement and fundraising. Within a matter of a few conversations and a few months into this new role, I was named project manager for the entire Pelotonia movement for our portion of the business. This was huge. I was in meetings with the CEO and CFO to talk about strategy and budget, and the budget, well, let's just say it was almost as much as I recruited a team of passionate leaders from other areas of the company who had their own stories and reason for wanting to kick cancer's butt. The ones I bonded with most were other daughters who had lost their daddies. My heart ached every time I was stopped in the hallways by someone else whose loved one had succumbed to some form of cancer. Still reeling from my own experience, I felt like I was taking over everyone's sadness and anger and grief and putting it on my shoulders to show cancer that it wasn't going to win. I had no qualms about being the face of the movement; I wanted to be the one holding the dagger when we hunted down cancer, dragged it to the ground, while begging for our mercy and compassion, and stabbed it through the heart like it had done to so many of my friends and family. I still had so much rage in my body from losing my dad that I didn't care what I had to do to make sure cancer could never hurt anyone again. I wanted that responsibility.

In August of 2011, I completed my first one hundred-mile bike ride from Columbus to Athens, Ohio. When I arrived in Logan, I stopped at the end of my parent's driveway, where my dad would have been sitting with my mom, son, and husband. I hugged my mom and told her I was going to make it, no matter how hot, dehydrated, and exhausted I was; I was going to make it. I had to make it and I had an angel with me to see to it that I did. Along the way, just short of one of the most intimidating and steep mountains that I swear could have been an ancestor of Mt. Everest—Okay, so there are no mountains in Ohio, but let me tell my story—a car pulled up next to me, and the familiar soothing sounds of Dave Matthews rolled out of the windows, "*To change the world, start with one step.*

However small, the first step is hardest of all." I knew that he was with me, pushing me forward; no way he was letting me get this far and not finish. As I walked my bike up the hill (don't judge me), I smiled from ear to ear with tears running down my flushed, filthy, sweaty, joyful cheeks because I knew I was going to make it. I also knew there would be the mother of all downhills coming up over the crest of this monstrosity, so it was a win-win on all accounts!

At the end of that Pelotonia fundraising season, our company raised $1.4 million, the most of any sub-peloton within our larger company, as well as the most among any sub-peloton in the entire event, **$1.4 million** to fund cancer research, every single penny of it. And it was all driven by my dad, our story, finding the silver lining on the darkest cloud of my life. We may not have gotten to write that letter to the doctors at the James like he originally wanted, but I made sure that he was able to repay them in some way, actually, over one million ways.

CHAPTER 12

All About the Boy

If anyone reading this book knows anything about me and my family, it is a foregone conclusion that Tyson should have his own chapter. At the time of writing this, he is a strong, free spirited, skinny nine-year-old boy with a style all his own. He's smart, he's funny, he's as charming as they make them, and he has all of the females in his life wrapped around his skinny little fingers. He also has attention deficit hyperactivity disorder (ADHD).

As I mentioned earlier, I could have known when I was pregnant that this boy was going to give me a run for my money. Think about when you go to an aquarium, one of those really big ones with the huge walls of glass holding back millions of gallons of water. You might think I would compare Tyson to the sharks in those tanks because you can constantly see them swimming around, looking like he owns the place, all in control. Nope. I want you to think about the eels that no one really pays attention to because they are in the background of all the other bright, colorful fish and coral and terrifying sharks. The eels are the ones swimming all around with nothing else to do, with no real purpose or cadence; they just flip and swim and flip and swim and flip and flip and swim and swim and swim and flip. That is what I felt in my stomach for the final four to five months of my pregnancy. He was either going to be a fish or a gymnast; I wasn't sure what to expect when the doctor showed him to me for the first time. Thankfully, he wasn't a fish, but with the height of his father and I, it's safe to say he won't be a gymnast, either.

The day we took Tyson home for the first time, we had no idea what was in store. Having a C-section, I was not to do any heavy lifting or regular walking up and down the stairs, which seemed pretty impossible since we lived in a split-level home with bedrooms and the bathroom on the second level. We made a trip to the grocery store to pick up food and formula and diapers and all that stuff you should probably get BEFORE you go to the hospital, but remember we did everything backward! To say the first night was a nightmare would not give it the justice it deserves. I'm not sure we slept a full four hours between the two of us. If we weren't getting up to change or feed him, we were lying in bed, leaping out of our pajamas every time we heard a "baby noise." No one told us about baby noises. I think that would have been important to know and maybe they didn't tell us because they had to find out the hard way and I guess maybe it's a rite of passage to new parents. Well, I still think it's rude that no one told us that these baby noises can sometimes be as nerve-racking as crying. It was timed so perfectly. The minute he would finally quiet down after finishing a bottle and we would crawl gently back into bed, quietly, BABY NOISE!

"Oh my gosh, is he okay? Is he still alive? What did we do to this child already? Oh no, it was just a cute little grunt or maybe a little gas relief. Okay, back to sleep. Wait, did you check to see if he was still breathing? Maybe his onesie is too tight. Why is he on his stomach? Don't you know he is supposed to sleep on his back? Well, now he's going to have SIDS and die; I can't go to sleep until this child learns to sleep all night on his back. Is it too hot in here? We should probably take off his blanket. But what if he pees and then he's too cold?"

It's funny to stop and think about the irrational thoughts that went through our minds that night and many nights to follow, but we all go through it and we live to tell the tale. One of the funniest things my husband has ever said to me happened on that first night. It was probably 3:00 a.m., right before our first SOS to the pediatrician on call because we didn't know how to make a baby stop crying, and he looked at me and said with a straight face, "People do this more than once?" We were both delirious at the time, so I can't even remember if I laughed or cried, but I think we knew that night that Tyson would be an only child!

Remember when I said I had a fairly easy pregnancy? Well, I now know why it was so routine because the days and months that followed were anything but routine with our new little bundle of joy.

I expect the 1:00 a.m., 3:00 a.m., 3:30 a.m., and 5:00 a.m. feedings and everything in between, but I had no idea how difficult it would really be to take care of a newborn baby. I am so grateful to my husband for staying home with me for the first week because I'm not so sure I would have made it without him. I was still recovering from the surgery with childbirth; I had to be reminded that I did have a major surgery with the C-section, coupled with sleep deprivation, confusion, and sleep deprivation (did I say that already?). I was mentally, physically, and emotionally exhausted. One of the best pieces of advice I received was to "sleep when he sleeps." At first, I thought that seemed silly. Isn't that the time you would want to use to clean the kitchen and take a shower? Taking a shower was a luxury on most days and a clean kitchen was the furthest thing from my mind. Oh, I slept when he slept, all right. I have plenty of pictures of each of us asleep with this angelic little monster sleeping on our chest on the couch.

But then, it happened. My husband had to go back to work. Wait, you mean I have to stay home by myself, all day, alone, with the baby? Do you think that's a good idea? It might not have been the best thing to do, at least in my mind, but he had to go to work and I had to put on my big girl pants and be a mommy. I tried so hard to do the best I could. I didn't want to bother anyone with my problems, so I didn't ask for nearly as much help as I should have. I wanted to show everyone, myself included, that I could do this and I wasn't going to burden someone because Tyson wouldn't sleep, eat, or stop crying. *Oh, the crying.* We both screamed and cried for our mommy when we were home alone. I felt like everything I did was wrong. He cried, I changed him. He cried, I fed him. He cried, I cried. He slept, I slept. The first few weeks felt like a battle of wills and I was against a more than formidable opponent.

I will never nominate myself for a "Mother of the Year" award, especially in those first few months. I am not proud of the yelling, screaming, and stomping I did when he just would not stop crying. I never laid my hand on him or did any physical harm to him; I could never forgive myself for that. I do confess to screaming at the top of my lungs on more occasions than I would like to admit, at times rivaling a crazed lunatic that should have been carted off to the insane asylum. It wasn't until later that I realized and acknowledged that I was a victim of postpartum depression. I had heard the term, but I had no clue what it truly meant until I stopped and looked in the mirror. I did not like this person who was looking back at me. How on earth could I be so upset and frazzled by this innocent, amazing, miraculous child? He wanted nothing from me but to be loved and taken care of, to be fed, burped, and put to sleep. But, to me, it felt like it was too much and I couldn't do anything to make him feel better. I was failing as a mother and it was only a few months. If I can't change a diaper and make him stop crying, how would I handle the important, more difficult things as he got older? Why had God given me a child who needed so much attention, so much more than I could apparently give him? Didn't he know that I was too busy building a career to have to drop everything and take care of a helpless infant? How would I ever get ahead if I had to push a baby stroller while running the corporate race? None of it made sense and I doubted that it ever would.

Once I went back to work after two months of "bonding" time with Tyson, my mom would drive to our house three days a week to babysit while Pat and I were at work. We live about forty minutes apart, and I didn't want her to drive back and forth every single day while also leaving my dad at home alone. We agreed to have her come to our house three days a week. She would take him home on Wednesday, and we would drive to their house to pick him up on Fridays after work. For two overly exhausted, under-rested, new parents, those overnights were the two most glorious days of the week. We had date nights on Wednesday nights at a local bar where we would sit and talk about our future dreams with our perfect family and our perfect jobs. Okay, who are we kidding? We talked about

Tyson the entire time and we revisited pictures on our phone over and over like we he had never seen them before. I texted my mom a few times a day and night to make sure everything was going well and that he wasn't too much of a bother. Even if he was a bother, which she assures me he wasn't, she wouldn't have told me anyway. I was conflicted with the whole arrangement from the very beginning. On one hand, it was great to have her available for us and to give us a few days a week to take care of ourselves and each other. On the other hand, I felt bad for the drive she was making and for leaving my dad at home alone all day. But I did appreciate the fact that my dad was getting to spend quality time with Tyson, not knowing how much time he would have with him. It pulled at my heartstrings because I didn't want to take advantage of my parents, even though they never saw it that way.

After about a year and a half, we knew we had to make the decision to put him in day care during the day and remove the burden from my mother. My dad had doctor appointments and treatments to go to and she wouldn't be able to take Tyson with her to the offices, although I have no doubt the nurses would have doted all over him. It was also time for us to grow up as parents and assume the responsibilities of being his parents, full-time, not five days a week. Besides, he needed to interact with other children, get those nasty baby germs to build his immunity, and learn to be without his mommy and daddy for a few hours a day. It was much easier said than done, we would quickly learn.

The next two years or so brought so much uncertainty, frustration, sadness, and guilt, but not for the reasons you might think. To cut to the chase, Tyson was kicked out of six day care facilities by the age of five. He didn't even make the cut at a local Montessori, which we learned was practically unheard of because they take the kids that (no one else will take) learn differently than other kids. You can only imagine the toll this took on our mental health, jobs, and our relationship. For a solid two years when my phone would ring at work, I would put my head down and sigh because I knew what was on the other end. Tyson was being sent home for not laying down for nap. Tyson was being sent home because he ran out of the room.

Tyson was being sent home because he tried to climb out a window. I'm not making that last one up, although I think someone else did. I was sure the next phone call I would receive would be my employer telling me not to worry about coming back the next day. We knew he was high energy and sometimes a little high maintenance, but could he really be that bad? There's no way anything he was doing warranted being sent home or being dismissed from the school.

If you are fortunate enough to be a parent of a spirited child (that's what the first book that I read called it), you know that it can be extremely taxing on every aspect of your life. For me, as frustrating as it was to have to leave work to retrieve him after another disaster at another school, it was more infuriating that the schools had no compassion, no concern for what they were putting our family through. It felt cold, unfair, and targeted, like a witch hunt. Was there a blacklist in our area at the day care facilities with our kid's picture with a warning not to enroll him? Would we have to leave the state to find someone to take him? Surely, he wasn't as bad as they made him out to be and I doubt he is the only high-energy kid they have ever seen. It broke my heart each time I walked in to pick him up and the manager would be standing at her office waiting to speak to me. In one of the last facilities, I'm not even sure if I said anything. I just walked in, grabbed Tyson and all of his belongings, and walked out, never to be seen again. Each time we had to explain to Tyson why he wasn't going back to that school the following week was just one more blow to the stomach that I wasn't prepared to handle. Thankfully, Tyson never really understood what was happening and I pray it doesn't affect him later in life, but we were rendered completely helpless with nowhere to turn.

Chapter 13

You and Me and ADD

After countless meetings with day care directors, sometimes involving begging and a few crocodile tears (I ain't too proud), and discussions with our pediatrician, we finally decided it was time to have Tyson tested. It was through this process that we realized what was happening, why he had been dismissed from the last six schools he was enrolled in. They knew more than we did at the time, but instead of helping us work through it, they washed their hands of us in favor of another paying student who wouldn't require as much attention.

The first talk with the doctor was not one I was mentally prepared for. I had a feeling that ADHD was going to come up in the conversation at some point; I had researched enough to know that was certainly on the table. The word I had not expected was autism. I burst into tears the minute the word left his mouth, without really understanding what an autism diagnosis would mean. Most of the stories of kids with autism (they are NOT autistic) center around those who are nonfunctioning, adult children who rely on their parents to care for them because they are unable to do so themselves. But autism is so much more than that. There is a medical "spectrum" that ranges from fully functioning individuals who may have social or speech difficulties that are not easily recognized by an outsider to low-functioning, nonverbal individuals who require physical and occupational therapy to function in society. The signs that Tyson had exhibited would likely put him closer to the fully functioning end, although it wasn't easy to grasp the labels that we were already trying to put on this child who was barely three years old.

Aside from his erratic behavior and difficulty sitting and following directions, Tyson did not communicate as well for his age and he struggled to make friends with other kids. Loud noises upset him; he would put his hands over his ears even when he was anticipating a disturbing sound. His speech was often hard to decipher and you could feel his frustration rise when we would ask him to repeat what he had said or just completely ignore the request because we didn't understand. A good night's sleep was unheard of which only elevated the other symptoms he was experiencing. I went as far as to sleep with him in his bed for almost a year just so we could all sleep at least a few hours a night. It might not have been the right decision, it didn't help my marriage, but I had to do whatever I could for my son. It was my role as a mother to take care of him, even if it meant sacrificing my own sleep patterns and comfort.

Tyson was officially diagnosed with attention deficit hyperactivity disorder at the ripe old age of three. Some thought he was too young to be given that prognosis, most folks didn't hesitate to share their opinions about ADHD with me, and well, you know what they say about opinions. But my husband and I felt confident that it was the right conclusion and about the treatment plan we had settled on with the doctor. Putting a child on medication at such a young age seems unfair and inhumane (according to conspiracy theorists), but we can attest to the necessity with Tyson. He would not be able to function or learn in any school setting if it were not for the medication he was prescribed. We were just happy to have answers and some sense of peace after the previous year we had endured. The diagnosis also made him eligible for different programs, including preschool in a neighboring school district, and an IEP (Individualized Education Plan), which we learned is crucial to set him up for success throughout his school years.

With this new learning, we made a huge leap of faith, probably a crazy one at the time, and moved to a new school district. What made it a little unnerving wasn't the actual idea of picking up and moving; we had already outgrown our starter home. It was the fact that we were going to be paying for two residences. The housing market was still reeling, although there were signs of life, but our neighborhood was not a desired location even for first-time home buyers. We only had a brief period after the diagnosis to move into the school district in time for Tyson to start preschool. There was no time to sell or even rent the house, so we bit the bullet and paid rent and a mortgage for almost seven months before we finally enlisted a realtor to help us rent the property. And then, the following year, we decided to move out of the rental into a new home, so then we had two mortgages and rent to worry about for a month or so while everything settled. When we do something, we go for it. This was to make sure our son was equipped with the best teachers who knew how to work with and encourage kids with similar learning abilities (I refuse to call it a disability). We may have been called foolish for putting ourselves at such financial risk, but you could never question the love and good intentions we had for Tyson.

While we were seemingly becoming adjusted to our new home and Tyson in his new school, I still had some lingering concerns of my own. Through the entire testing, diagnosis, and treatment development plan with Tyson, I recognized and empathized with some of the internal conflict he battled unconsciously. My mother, the nostalgic one of the family (don't you dare call her a hoarder!), pulled out my grade cards from elementary school from an old box hidden deep in a cabinet in their family room. I was an "A" student and had perfect attendance through about sixth grade, a teacher's dream. Well, I would have been if it weren't for the comments at the end of every grade card for every period for every grade from kindergarten through sixth grade. "Tez is always disrupting others when she is done with her work." "Great student, but she can't sit still." "She cannot keep her mouth shut." Now, this was obviously long before political correctness ruled the land, so the last comment might seem a little harsh and rude in today's educational setting, but if the shoe fits, I will wear it and wear it well.

Those same habits haunted me through junior high, high school, and even college, as I fought to focus on anything for longer than a few minutes. My mind goes 100 mph and my mouth even faster. I interrupt people in a conversation a minimum of three times. I consider myself reasonably intelligent, not quite a Mensa scholar, but I underachieved in my collegiate experience. I have no problem picking up on something, I am a quick learner, and I love to learn new things. My Achilles heel is that I rush through everything I do to get it done so I can move on to the next challenge. For some, that might feel like an admirable quality, but it's not so commendable when you present inaccurate or downright incorrect information in a meeting with senior-level executives because you rushed to get it done. That is just not acceptable in any level of an organization or company, that is, unless you are a meteorologist and you get to keep your job even though your forecast is wrong seventy-five percent of the time. Throw on top of that my astute ability to procrastinate and disaster is almost destined to ensue.

The week of my thirty-ninth birthday, I was diagnosed with ADD, seriously, thirty-nine. I'm sure I have had it all my life, but once I saw myself in Tyson, I knew I had to do something. I had just started a new job and I didn't want to continue down the same path making the same mistakes, jumping from one job to the next before I could make the final mistake that would send me to the unemployment line. What kind of example would I be setting for my son if I didn't take responsibility and accountability for my own damaging behaviors?

For years I had an unrelenting haze that occupied the front portion of my forehead between my eyebrows. I was unable to concentrate, and when I was finally able to hold my focus, I would become totally fixated on something, almost to the point of obsession. I hated to be wrong, still do, but sharing what I thought were amazing analyses only to find out they were completely erroneous and misguided sent me spiraling out of control. The only person harder on myself than me is, well, me. I would dwell on a mistake for at least the next three projects and with each one my confidence dwindled into virtual nonexistence. I would shy away from taking on something new to avoid the subsequent inevitable catastrophe.

That diagnosis was a turning point in my life, specifically in my career. After several trials of stimulants versus non-stimulant medications with a psychiatrist, I landed on Concerta. I have never been in a better place. It was like someone turned on a high-powered industrial sized fan and blew away the film that had been covering my brain for all these years. I became a new person, a better employee and a smarter partner virtually overnight. I have grown to be someone whom others look to for guidance or as a sounding board for ideas and strategies. It feels good; it feels damn good to be where I should have been all along. I just had to set aside my pride and ego and admit that I needed help, something that was not exactly in my wheelhouse.

Prior to every flight on every airline, the flight attendants advise you in case of emergency to put your oxygen mask on before assisting other passengers. I know I'm not the only one, but my first inclination would be to make sure my son has his breathing mask on all nice and snug with oxygen flowing freely through his tube to his precious little lungs before I even consider doing the same for myself. I am his mother; that would be totally irresponsible to take oxygen from my baby's lungs in favor of saving my own life. No, it is quite the opposite. With ADD, I have had to learn to take care of myself first, keeping up on my medications, following up with the psychiatrist, and getting enough sleep, before I can even begin to help Tyson figure out his life. If he watches me doing the opposite of what I am telling him to do, he will either emulate what I am doing or he will lose his trust and respect for me because I'm not walking what I'm talking. And this boy is like a damn elephant, he doesn't forget a thing, so he will call me out in a New York minute if I'm off my game. No one wants to be called out by a nine-year-old.

Sharing an ADD/ADHD diagnosis with Tyson allows me to bond with him and empathize with him in ways that few others can. The doctors can prescribe his medication, his teachers can provide him with appropriate accommodations, but I can show him how to thrive, not just survive with ADHD, by setting the example and following through with everything I do. Before I took the step to address my own deficiencies, I was trying to "fix" him, to figure out how to make him a normal little boy. Now I have learned to embrace and appreciate our distinct way of coping with an outside world that has no idea what to do with thinkers and dreamers like us. He never has to feel alone because there is someone living under the same roof who can walk with him every painful, confusing, enlightening, stimulating step of the way.

CHAPTER 14

Check Out the New Joint

When people find out that I played basketball at a Division 1 college, they immediately think, "That's great, saved you all that money in student loans." While that is true, my thirty plus years of strenuous athletics costs me in a much more significant way, my health. Playing sports and exercising are great for stress relief, weigh maintenance, teamwork, and self-esteem, but it is hell on our bodies. Just think about it and it's logical. Our bodies were not made to run miles and miles while jumping up and down and cutting from side to side at the drop of a dime. Sure, we have to exercise in order to keep our bodies and our minds in shape, but I doubt we were ever intended to play thirty game seasons on top of three-to-four-hour practices in addition to off-season training on hard, unforgiving concrete or unpliable plywood floors. I am a living proof of that.

After five surgeries on my left knee and one ACL reconstruction on my right knee, I was still trying to prolong my glory years by playing basketball, volleyball, and softball as if I was still in my twenties. I just couldn't give up that part of my life. Athletics defined me. It was something I was good at and I wouldn't let anyone take that away from me. I would play pickup basketball or sand volleyball games and then wake up the next morning feeling like someone was doing target practice shooting hot, fiery bullets at my knees. In my mind, I was twenty; in my knee, I was seventy-five. Those are the exact words of my orthopedic doctor who told me several times to take up golf. When he did my ACL reconstruction on my good knee, he advised me the only reason he was doing it was so I could walk; otherwise he would just leave it torn to teach me a lesson. *Ha, very funny, doc. Now, give me my pain meds and get out of my way; I have a softball game.*

The pain had finally gotten to be too much. I had started to lose feeling in the left side of my body, all the way from my back through my hips and ending at my toes. I was numb. It almost felt as if I didn't even have lower extremities because they served no purpose. Now, clearly that didn't stop me from continuing to subject myself to even more torture-playing sports year-round; that's what Aleve is for. But I had enough. The injections had stopped working, the steroids were useless—and they made me a raving lunatic!—and I wanted my life back. I attribute my long-term depression to the chronic pain I had been living with for almost twenty years. I tried to explain that to my husband time after time, but I don't think you can really grasp what that means until you go through it. His response was always, "Well, if you are so depressed and in so much pain, how can you go play six games of volleyball every week?" Hmm, he has a point there; let me get back to you on that. I had depression from the pain and on top of that I had anxiety because I knew that at some point I was going to be forced to quit playing sports and give in Father Time and let go. I was always in control of my life and I sure as hell wasn't going to let someone tell me when it was time to quit doing something.

In October of my fortieth year, I had a total knee replacement of my left. I mean, even the initials are the same as my name (TKR); it was a match made in titanium heaven. Not many doctors will even engage in a conversation about replacement until you are at least fifty and even that is a stretch. Studies show that joint replacements have a life span of about twenty years, on the long side, ten to fifteen on average. Thankfully, I found a surgeon who felt sorry for me and could see how much pain I was in and he scheduled me for surgery as soon as I wanted to get it done. The x-rays of my arthritic knee probably helped a bit, too. My kneecap had slid way off course and I had bone that had started going rogue and grew in places it wasn't supposed to simply because there was nothing else there. There's this stuff called cartilage that we have in our knees that acts as a buffer between our bones, similar to the oil that we put in cars, so the pounding we put our bodies through doesn't cause a serious malfunction. I didn't have any of that and hadn't had any since Clinton was in the White House in the Oval Office with Monica with a cigar and a blue dress. By this time, the other Clinton was running for president against a guy who used to host a reality TV show, grabs women by their, ahem, lady parts, and owns the Miss America pageant. Boy how the times had changed.

I had heard from others who had total knee and hip replacements that it was the best decision they ever made and they wish they had done it sooner. Now, remember, these surgeries are usually reserved for slightly more seasoned individuals, typically over the age of fifty to fifty-five. In my case, this was the first time I had the offer to do the surgery and I was not about to pass it up! Although I figured it would alleviate some of the shooting pains in my left side of my body, I had no preconceived expectation going into the surgery. I was a little stressed about having yet another surgery, as I felt like I had to be nearing my quota for a number of times being put under by anesthesia, and I literally almost passed out in the doctor's office as he explained the procedure to me. But I had to give it a try; there was no turning back. I wanted to feel normal again, I had no idea what that even meant anymore. I just wanted to be able to walk without feeling fireworks going off in my knee with every little step. This was my only option.

As I write this, I am about nine months post-op and I feel like a brand new person. Making the decision to have the surgery will probably go down as one of the smartest decisions I have made in my forty-one years. I haven't had that many of those, so the bar was set really low! When I say that I have absolutely no pain, I am not exaggerating and I'm not on the funny medicine to make me say that, either! The results are nothing short of a miracle. I can walk and I can jump out of bed in the morning without propping myself up on the wall or anything close to my bed. And, don't tell my doctor (sorry, doc!), but I can play volleyball and softball, too. I did give up basketball, so it's not like I didn't heed his warnings; I have just learned how to play "smarter." When you get to a certain age, you learn how to play with more finesse rather than skill, basically you learn how to be lazy yet still effective! More importantly, my depression? Gone. Even though I can't play sports to the level I used to play and I can't go out and run (that was NOT a tough one for me to give up), I can still be active and lead a normal life. That is something never in a million years thought that I would be able to say again. My knee feels amazing. My mind and soul feel even better.

It was another challenge during the week of my surgery that sent my life spinning out of control. Good thing I had that new knee to balance on.

CHAPTER 15

Scars to Prove It

"I'm leaving." Those were the two words emblazoned on my Samsung phone that jumped right off the screen like a 3D horror movie and shot a dagger through my heart. My husband had just left to take Tyson to a soccer game and I was settling in on the couch with my aunt to watch the Ohio State football game. I can't even tell you who they were playing because I'm not sure I watched any of the game. He seemed flustered as he rushed Tyson out the door, and that's typical since it takes an army to get that boy out the door in a timely manner! Since I was only about three days post-op, I wasn't allowed to leave the house and I had to limit my trips up and down the stairs. I was also struggling with some "complications" from the pain meds I had been popping for those three days and things just weren't moving inside like they were supposed to. I will save you the details and the illustrations, but if you have ever had surgery and stayed on Percocet or Vicodin for any amount of time, you know what I'm talking about!

I had sent a text to Pat to ask if he was okay and to tell him thank you for taking care of me, Tyson, and everything around the house while I was laid up. I just assumed he was frazzled because he was doing all of this as well as keeping things together at work. He had taken the entire week off to help because he would now have drop off and pick up duty for Tyson; he would need to help me get up and down the stairs, all of the usual restrictions they place you on after surgery. He had also been working his butt off on a grant application at work and I knew that he was stressed and exhausted.

We texted (yes, I said texted) back and forth for the entire length of the soccer game until he walked in the door. My aunt excused herself rather quickly, and the next few hours and days became so awkward and tense and disheartening as I still had to recover from surgery and we had to put up a good show for Tyson. Thank God he never saw or heard us fighting through any of this. Most of our disagreements came through texts and e-mails, and we never brought any of this in front of him. It worked out that way, but it was only because we were too selfish and cowardly to have a real conversation without a screen in front of our faces.

He stayed in the house for the next two nights, sleeping in our bed upstairs while I was sleeping downstairs on the couch or in the guest room. We had planned it that way since I couldn't go up and down the stairs and I assumed my sleeping patterns would be all over the place, depending on the pain. I was also still waiting for a visit from the number 2 fairy, and she was taking her good old time, while I was balled up in the fetal position on the floor feeling like a cement mixer. And, yeah, it also felt like concrete when all was said and done!

The second night following his revelation, I went to bed and it took me a few hours to fall sleep as I was texting a few friends about what was going on and what I should do. I sat with my thoughts for a little while; I googled "how to get my husband to stay" over a million times looking for any sort of hope that I could get him to change his mind. I also read my Bible. I was still getting familiar with books and passages, knowing which ones apply to which areas of my life, but reading through some of the sites I found in my desperate search, I discovered many references to God's wishes for marriage and I prayed hard for those things to transpire. The next morning after Pat dropped Tyson off to school, he came back home and sat on the couch next to me. It felt as if he was looking at me with pity in his eyes knowing the conversations we had over the past few days and that I couldn't even get up off the couch to take a drive or just get away from my reality. He asked, "Do you need anything?"

"No," I said. Even if I did need anything, I sure wasn't going to ask him to do it for me. I would get it myself if I really needed it. But then, I had the strangest feeling come over me and what I said next was as much of a shock to me as it was to him. I looked at him and said, "Actually, I do need something. I need you to leave." I have heard of out-of-body experiences, but I have never experienced one myself. I had a five-second conversation in my head, like what in the world did you just say? Did I say that? I wanted to look around the room to see if there was someone else standing behind me, half expecting to see a ventriloquist with his hand up my back.

He looked back with a confused look and said, "You mean now?"

"Yes, now."

We still have the first house we bought together; it's about five miles from our current home. We had rented it out several times, that is another book all its own, and we were working with a property manager to get it repaired for another rental. The day before, he had asked me several times if he should call the property manager to tell him we weren't going to rent it because one of us would be living in it. I had no plans of leaving my home, so if anyone was going to move into that house, it would have to be him. But I also didn't want him asking me what I thought his next move should be. I think that kind of went out the window when he made the decision to tell me he wanted to leave.

He then said that he didn't want or need to leave right away because I still needed him to help around the house while I rehabilitated my knee. Remember, this was my seventh surgery, so this wasn't my first rodeo. As I'm sure you have already learned, I can be a little hardheaded and stubborn and on occasion I may do things against doctor's wishes. I wasn't worried about getting myself up and down the stairs at this point. I would figure it out. I am an old pro at using crutches; they fall so perfectly into my armpit area, like they were always meant to be there. I can take care of myself. If not, my mom, aunt, and cousin were very willing and able to come take care of anything else I needed. I didn't need him sitting there staring at me with puppy dog eyes feeling sorry for me, not sorry because of the pain from my knee, sorry for the pain that had now shifted to my heart. It was embarrassing, demoralizing, and I refused to show any sign of weakness or helplessness.

Over the next few days, I had to watch this man come in our house and pack up everything that was his and pack it away in his car to take back to the house that we had worked so hard to move out of. Looking back, it was almost symbolic: he moved backward, while I'm trying to move forward. Most people probably do these painful activities while the other person is out of the house, either at work or just out of sight, saving the other from further humiliation and heartache. Nope, I watched every single shirt float from the closet upstairs to the back seat of his car. I watched each pair of shoes walked right out of the house, every single thing. My half-empty walk-in closet now felt as expansive as cowboy stadium, while my world felt like it was closing in on me. I sat in that closet and cried. Actually, I wailed and screamed and begged God to show me a way to bring him home. I promised that I would never ask for another thing if I could just have my family back together. He knows the drill; He's heard it all before.

There is so much to talk about from those nine months of separation, but it's not what this book is supposed to be about. I did not write this book to bash my husband or make him pay by airing our dirty laundry. I was moved to share my story, to share the trials I have been through with others who may have lost their way in their own storm. Reliving all the unpleasant events of the last few months of my marriage would be disrespectful and unfair to the man I shared the last fourteen years of my life with, our nine-year-old son, and the man that asked me to write the book in the first place. I will share my feelings through this tumultuous, confusing time of my life, but I will not downplay nor dismiss his feelings or try to analyze them because it is not my place to do that. I may not owe him much, but I do owe him that respect.

The Aftermath

It's hard to imagine ever smiling again while you are amid a significant trial. I had nine months to get used to my husband no longer being a part of my life, at least not in the way he had always been, but up until our court date, we were still technically married. Now, I have an ex-husband. I have resorted to calling him Tyson's dad because I can't bring myself to say his name, it burns like hot lava all the way from the deepest part of my stomach through to the very last fiber on the tip of my tongue. When I went on a solo trip to North Carolina for a writer's conference, I walked through uptown Charlotte and picked up real estate listing magazines, something he and I always did when we visited a new city. I have places that we used to go to that I can't even bear to step into anymore. His face is everywhere I look in my house. He is still sitting in HIS recliner in front of the television; I can't even bring myself to sit in that chair, fourteen years of stupid, ridiculously corny inside jokes that aren't funny anymore and wouldn't make a bit of sense to anyone but us. A home that we built together with our blood, sweat, and tears and a few beers, it's all gone. And I'm just supposed to "get over it." What does that even mean?

Everyone tells me how strong a woman I am and that I shouldn't let this get me down. Truth be told, I didn't want to be strong at the time and anytime in the foreseeable future. I wanted to scream and cry and tell everyone to leave me alone while I grieve, because I am still grieving, and it is no different than grieving the loss of a loved one. The last thing on my mind right now was being strong and getting over it. I wanted to crawl in bed and ugly cry until my face was blood red and raw from my warm salty tears that had been hibernating since I lost my dad in 2011. These tears are reserved for death, not for the life I never wanted to give up. To hell with my strength. Does my strength mean I have to roll over and accept it and say, "Oh well, what's next?" I sure hope not because that just was not going to happen. God willing, I will wake up tomorrow and the next day and the next, and I will move forward with whatever this new normal turns out to be. But I was not okay. I didn't feel like I would ever be okay and I wanted someone to tell me I wouldn't be okay. And that itself should be okay. All these years, people have told me what I wanted to hear to make me feel good and confident about myself, but when I really wanted someone to agree with me, I couldn't find a single soul.

Others who have been through divorce tell me that there is someone out there for me and that they were able to find a love that has been better than they have ever imagined with someone else. He was my someone and I don't want to think about anyone else. Besides, I'm waiting for the sign that I ordered from Amazon (of course I'm a prime member and they sell EVERYTHING) to wear around my neck that says, "Damaged goods, selling as-is, lots of miles, but loyal and reliable." Isn't that how this works? Won't people know as soon as they see me that I'm divorced and my husband left me because I wasn't good enough for him anymore? Won't they realize and stop and stare at me with their kids saying, "Honey, that's a divorced woman. You don't want to end up like her. You don't want to be alone when you are forty-one."

My marriage is now technically "dissolved." That makes it sound like it never even happened. It would also lead you to believe that it has the same effects of an Alka-Seltzer in that it can help to cure my upset stomach, or in this case my heart. *Fizz, fizz, plop, plop, your marriage was a flop.*

Instead of preparing to celebrate our tenth wedding anniversary, our fifteenth year together, I now have two other dates to add to my planner: October 10, the day he moved out, and July 18, the day our marriage was officially over. In October I was blindsided, t-boned by a Mack truck that was being pushed from behind by a 747. I would rather have been punched in the gut by Connor McGregor, at least then I would have had a scar to show for it and an interesting story to tell, or maybe even a few bucks from a lawsuit. Nope, this scar is way down deep beneath the surface, a place that I had tried to hide for so long. I never wanted to feel my heart break, so I refused to open it up to let anyone for a long time. Even after fourteen years, I don't know that I let him in totally for fear that this exact thing might happen. Vulnerability is nowhere in my internal dictionary; even typing the word gives me a panic attack. If I'm not vulnerable, not showing all my cards, no one can beat me. I can only beat myself by making a senseless bet or throwing the wrong card. I have always felt that by letting someone in, that person would use my vulnerability against me and leave me, even more broken than when they met me. I was broken for too long; I longed to be made whole again. So, I did it. I let him in and let him see me, all of me, the good, the bad, the perfectly broken fragments of my soul that just needed the right artist to come along and sculpt me into a better version of myself. But I also saw all of him, too. I thought I knew him better than I know myself, at times, apparently not this time.

CHAPTER 16

The "Other" Man

During the time that I was watching one relationship morph into something that was barely a vague version of its former self, another relationship was being rekindled and reborn.

On Christmas day of 2016, I gave my life back to Christ. I had been baptized with my family when my father died, but I felt that was only a superficial act to make my mom and dad happy, dad's dying wish of sorts. I had been growing in my faith since I started going to church in August and it played a significant role in my reaction to the events that transpired in the following months. It's no question that I am an emotional person; I don't have a good enough poker face to win a game of old maid. If this situation had happened one year prior, I would not have been in a healthy spiritual condition to handle a major catastrophe like divorce.

I have always believed in God. I like to watch the *Big Bang Theory* series on television, but I don't believe that is how we arrived at this life on earth. Look around each day and see the miracles that exist; there are no scientific or worldly explanations to some of life's greatest mysteries. If I had to name my belief, I would have called myself a casual Christian. I believed, but I didn't go out of my way to learn what I was believing in and how that belief could change my life. I had also committed enough of my own sins in forty-one years that I just assumed I would go to heaven, but I might be staying at the Holiday Inn instead of the Ritz-Carlton of heaven. I did enough to get there, but not enough to be in the 1 percent of heaven, similar to how I lived my life here on earth.

With the risk of being called crazy, dramatic, or irrational, I will share one of the supernatural experiences that I had in the preliminary stages of this new faith walk. Trust me, if it didn't happen to me and I didn't witness it with my own twenty-twenty eyes, I would call myself crazy too. This was one of the turning points of my journey, that point where you realize that He is talking to you and He will do whatever it takes to make sure you are listening. He will do it in ways that only He can do and ways that only you can see. If it doesn't make sense, and you wouldn't dare tell someone else for fear they may have you committed, it's probably Him.

I was driving to work with an overabundance of things running through my mind; alone time in my car became my worst enemy. I was still in the process of learning how to pray and how to listen when He was ready to tell me something. I was frustrated because I hadn't seen Him move in my life and hadn't heard His voice that I hear others talk about. Had He forgotten about me? Am I not "Christian" enough for God to intercede on my behalf in my trials? As much as I was getting comfortable with the idea of God, what I wasn't comfortable with was what I had felt with His lack of communication. *Careful what you ask for.*

As I made a left-hand turn at a stop light, I saw a car to my right that looked like it had just crashed into a telephone pole. The pole was intact and unblemished, but the front end of the car was sitting right up against it. The way it was sitting in the parking lot; there was no good reason for the car to be positioned where it was except if it was an accident. I realized there was a driver in the car, leaned back in the seat, but I couldn't tell if he was hurt, stunned, or just absorbing what had just occurred. Why was no one stopping? This was 8:30 a.m. during the work week on a busy street and no other driver had stopped to help. Is it really that much more important for people to get to work on time than it is to help a fellow human being? There was no safe place for me to stop, so I decided to drive up the road to the next driveway so that I could safely do a U-turn and go back to help this potentially injured man. This all happened within a span of three to four minutes, at the very most. I figured by this time someone would have surely stopped or called 911 to get the police or paramedics involved, so I was expecting to hear sirens.

When I got back to the spot, the car was gone, G-O-N-E, gone. I drove by looking, wondering if I had misjudged where it happened, so I continued a little further. Nope. I turned and drove back by the spot again, still gone. There were no police, no ambulance, and no car. The only thing that remained was the telephone pole. I pulled into a lot just beyond the spot and sat in my car, speechless. I had no idea what had just happened and I tried to explain it away with every scenario I could think of. Maybe he really was just sitting in the car checking a text or an address because he was lost. But, why was he pulled up right next to the pole? Maybe he hit the pole, but he ran because he was high or drunk and didn't want to get arrested. But, I didn't pass the car when I turned around and headed back to the scene. He would not have had the time to pull away, drive into oncoming traffic in the opposite direction without me seeing him. I continued to drive to work, dumbfounded, confused, and at this point laughing at what had just materialized.

A few months later, I had a similar experience, but this time it was after work. I had planned to leave by 5:00 p.m. on this day, but a late meeting kept me in the office until almost 5:30 p.m. As I pulled out of the lot, I saw a car on the side of the road with the driver outside, concerned, chatting on the phone. I looked closer and realized that it was a friend of mine who I had some rough dealings with about a year ago. We hadn't talked in over a year, but I had to see if everything was okay. I would never forgive myself if I didn't do something. Again, not in a safe place to stop, I made a right turn and an immediate left turn to go back to see if I could do anything. As with the first story, this all happened in a span of three minutes or less. When I arrived at the spot, she was gone. Where her car was sitting, I would have seen her pull away and there was simply no trace of her. Was I losing my mind or was someone trying to get my attention?

Looking back on these instances, I believe the purpose was twofold. First, my faith and my obedience were being tested to see if I would perform my duties to serve others while He was working in the background on the things I had prayed for. The easiest thing to do when our lives don't go as we had planned is turn our backs on anyone else who might need our help, friends, family, or even strangers. We are so entrenched in our own feelings, how we think we have been wronged and left behind, that we believe we have nothing to offer and that we have no obligation to offer. Truth is, it is the exact opposite.

Second, I believe that God was tired of my questioning His plan and His process, the timing of His movement in my circumstances. I can just imagine Him sitting on His throne looking down on me and saying, "You want proof? You want to see what I can do? Watch this." Supernatural interventions—many have heard of them, but some never experience them or recognize them when they happen. I have not had anything nearly that deliberate for a few months, but He has found other ways to talk to me. I won't share all my secret conversation methods, some things do have to remain between myself and the Father, but He talks to me in numbers and semi-trucks. Don't judge me. Yes, I said, semi-trucks, and I'm not divulging that inside joke with God until I see where it leads. Trust me, when it happens, you will be among the first to know.

They say that the church is no longer what it used to be; people have turned their backs on God, Jesus, the church, and one another. The minute someone makes the decision to turn their lives over to Christ, they are met with much scrutiny, mockery, and sometimes outright disdain. But why? Why do we find it so hard to be happy for another human being who is putting their trust and faith in someone or something? What is worse, believing in something or believing in nothing at all? During one of the first sermons that I attended with my new church family, my pastor said something so simple, yet so profound that I think about it almost every day. He said, "I don't know about you, but when I die, I would rather believe that there is a heaven and then find out that there isn't when I get there than not believe and find out there is one." Do you want to be the one standing outside the gates, gazing, envious of your friends and family members who believed and are now reaping the harvest that they sowed here on earth? I know I'm not making that mistake. Are you?

CHAPTER 17

When Practice Pays Off

Rejoice in the Lord always. I will say it again: Rejoice! 5 Let your gentleness be evident to all. The Lord is near. 6 Do not be anxious about anything, but in every situation, by prayer and petition, with thanksgiving, present your requests to God. 7 And the peace of God, which transcends all understanding, will guard your hearts and your minds in Christ Jesus. **Philippians 4:4**

That was the first scripture that I felt was written just for me; He was talking to me. And how do I know He was talking to me? He sent that scripture, or some variation of that scripture, to me about ten times within a five-day period. I had chosen this verse to discuss in Bible study and one of my fellow church members had chosen the very same verse. I read it the next morning in a devotional. I received an email with it from my pastor's wife that same morning. I was listening to a book on CD in my car and it was quoted within the first five minutes. I also visited a residence later that week and the address? It was 44 Sky View Place. I think He was trying to tell me something.

"Do not be anxious about anything, but in every situation, by prayer and petition, with thanksgiving, present your requests to God."

After my husband left me, my emotions, confidence, and self-worth were all over the place. I struggled to find anything that made sense, and frankly, I struggled to find someone to talk to who could tell me what to do next or what NOT to do next. I love my friends and family and I wanted to talk to them about everything I was going through, because many of them have been through relationship issues or divorces of their own, but none of it helped. Of course, they wanted to support me and comfort me, but it also made me feel like they felt sorry for me. They wanted to make me feel better and they would tell me everything that I wanted to hear or that he didn't deserve me and I could do better. That's not what I wanted or even needed to hear. As much as he hurt me when he walked out that door, I didn't want to hear anyone say one bad word about him. Although I didn't agree with the things he had said to me or with his reasons for wanting to leave, I also refused to think of him as a bad person and I tried to stick up for him as much as I could. Even that didn't help, as much as I tried.

I believe that my timing around returning to church was planned long before I even thought about it. As I said in the beginning of the book, I always believed in God and that we will go to heaven when we die (well, some of us will!), but I honestly never stopped to think about what He does with us while we are still on earth. Sure, I hear stories of supernatural miracles of people surviving deadly car crashes or being cured of cancer after being told by doctors that there is simply no hope, but I didn't think he cared or wasted his time with the "little things." Why on earth would God help me get a new career or calm my nerves when He has much bigger things to take care of like world peace or planning the next natural disaster? In all my years of practice, it never even occurred to me to turn to Him first to talk about His plans for my life or to understand the lessons He was trying to teach me. If I had done that, I can almost guarantee the theme of this would have taken on a much different tone.

One of the first things I learned that God was trying to teach me was patience. Patience is not in my regular vocabulary and it nearly gives me a panic attack just thinking about having to wait and be patient for something. But that impatience is a nagging side effect to the real culprit which is being a control freak. I feel I must control everything, e-v-e-r-y-thing. I hate surprises. I cannot stand when someone makes a plan that we have already agreed on and then decide they want to change at the last second. I asked God more times than I can even begin to count for grace and mercy regarding patience and letting go in my resurrection period. I still don't have a good grasp on it, and I fall off the wagon more times than I would like to admit, but I at least know that I can ask Him for that grace and for help in improving on that aspect of my life, which really is the root cause to much of what I have experienced in my life. Looking back, most of the issues that I endured were somewhat self-inflicted, not consciously, but certainly because of my inability to go with the flow.

The second of my sins that is just as hard for me to change as giving up control is learning to forgive others who have wronged me. I used to believe I was the type of person who couldn't hold a grudge, but the older I have gotten, the more I realize that is no longer a strength of mine. It can be as simple as someone cutting me off in traffic or someone jumping in front of me at the line in the grocery store. If you do me wrong, it's hard for you to get back in my good graces. And sometimes, you don't even have to be the one who has done something to me. As in the scenarios above, I tend to hang onto things way too long after they have happened and then I take it out on the next few people I see after the incident. It just spirals out of control from there. Most times when I would get home after work, my son and husband would take the brunt of the anger I held onto from the guy that cut me off on the on-ramp to 70W at 7:00 a.m. that morning.

It's a fact of life that we all sin, every single day of our lives. God did not make us to be perfect. Well, He kind of did, but this couple named Adam and Eve ate an apple, realized they were naked, and ruined it for the rest of us. But despite our daily misguided actions and words, He still offers and guarantees us His unfailing love, grace, and forgiveness (John 3:16). He made the most selfless sacrifice for each of us, the ones who screw up His divine plans on a daily basis, and offered His son for execution. Now, I don't know about you, but if any of you reading this book ever do something crazy, and someone has to take the fall for your actions, ain't no way I am giving up my son to a band of ruffians for your indiscretions. Really, think about that and what it means for your life. He loved us so much that He let His very own innocent son die on a cross, huge spikes piercing his hands and feet, so that you and I could live freely and not be persecuted for our sins. I think we owe Him a little something in return, don't you? And all He asks is for us to love Him and talk to Him and trust in Him. Sounds like a pretty fair request, to me. So why is it so hard for me to forgive someone who has hurt my feelings if He can so unequivocally offer it to me just by my asking through repentance in prayer?

Along with forgiving others, we must also learn to forgive ourselves, which I am also working on. We live so much of our lives in the past and the future that we never get to enjoy what we have right in front of us today. We relive past hurts and disappointments and we look forward to being out of certain seasons of our lives that we don't appreciate what today is trying to teach us. Every day is not full of unicorns and rainbows unless you are a unicorn, and if you are, you probably aren't reading this book because you have no trials in your life. There is not one verse or scripture in the Bible that says life will be easy and we shouldn't expect any trials in our lives. What it does say is that when trials do emerge and things don't go as planned, you can lean on Him and He will guide you through. It also does not say He will click His heels together and take you back to never, never land; it says that He will GUIDE and support you. That was one of the hardest things I have had to comprehend mainly from the loss of my father to cancer and, now, losing my husband to divorce. If God is so good and wonderful and loves me so much, why on earth would He let my father die? Doesn't He know how much that hurt? Why would he promote something like divorce? Doesn't he hate divorce?

*And we know that in all things God works for the good of those who love him, who have been called according to his purpose. **Romans 8:28***

There are a few words that I had to learn to be comfortable with through the most recent trials in my life, words that slide off my tongue in everyday conversation, without giving a second thought to what they really mean. Along with patience and vulnerability, I also had to learn grace, mercy, gratitude, humility, and faith. Those are some pretty heavy words that, if used in the wrong context and taken completely for granted, can send you careening down the very mountain that you thought you were just about to conquer. All it takes is losing your focus from the end goal for one second, to go beyond the path where the sign says, "DO NOT ENTER." While there may not be a detailed map marked with check-in points to get you to where you need to go, there are rest stops along the way to check your progress and course-correct where necessary. You also have your very own tour guide with you every stop of the way, all you must do is ask, and He wants you to ask.

Anyone that has been through any divorce or relationship break up knows that being able to forgive the other person is one of the toughest battles you will ever fight through. If you have been able to forgive and forget and move on like nothing happened, please send me an email with your secret. Matter of fact, you should be writing a book! For the first few weeks after he moved out, all I could think about was how selfish he was being by leaving his family, not looking back for one second. How could you turn from someone whom I loved very much to my arch nemesis in what felt like a split second? I swore up and down that I would never speak to him again; I wouldn't give him one thing that he wanted from the house that he left behind. I was bound and determined to make him regret leaving and I was not about to roll over and beg him for his forgiveness for whatever it was he thought I did to him. I'm supposed to forgive him? What kind of sick game is this? That's when I was introduced to the word grace.

Grace is most times referred to as "simple elegance or refinement of movement"; think of a ballet dancer as they seem to float across the stage, effortlessly, gracefully. Where I grew up in Southeastern Ohio, if someone called you "grace," it meant you were clumsy and moved about as graceful as a penguin on a tightrope. I've never seen a penguin on a tightrope, but I imagine it's anything but graceful. Christians describe grace as receiving the favor and blessings of God. What is missing from this short definition is the phrase "even when we don't deserve it." God extends grace to us every single moment of every single day. Every waking breath that you take is grace. Every close call you have with a fatal car accident or the recovery from an injury or illness, that's grace. Although the definitions don't have a clear connection to one another, you can see where the two are intermingled in their meaning and their importance. Receiving God's grace can be described as a beautiful, effortless refining of movement, simple elegance. He doesn't have to give it to us; He wants to give it to us, even if we fail to reach His expectations on a daily basis. We were never created to be perfect. You can blame Adam and Eve for that. I blame Adam, but I might be biased since I'm coming through a divorce! Who are you and I to deny someone grace because they have wronged us, or we feel they have wronged us? There is no marriage or friendship handbook laid out that says what is expected as you enter a relationship, so it's a foregone conclusion that humans are going to fail us no matter how hard they try not to. We set them up for failure with unrealistic, uncommunicated expectations and then act surprised when they betray or hurt us. On the other hand, there is a handbook called the Bible that has been given to us as we think about our spiritual relationship with God. There is no gray area; He tells us exactly what He expects from us, how often He expects it, and even what we should expect from Him. There is no sugarcoating; there are no false or broken promises. He never tells us that anything is going to be perfect in our lives. We must not only learn to accept grace from God and from others, we must also unapologetically extend our grace to those who have wronged us. If you are unable to do that, you will never be ready to receive the gifts that are waiting for you.

The point is this: whoever sows sparingly will also reap sparingly, and whoever sows bountifully will also reap bountifully. **2 Corinthians 9:6**

Going hand in hand with our need to accept as well as offer grace is the act of mercy. The way I look at it is that grace is the gift that is given to someone who is being forgiven for a mistake committed against another. Mercy is the absence of punishment for the perpetrator, when it certainly feels justified or warranted. It is impossible to give someone mercy without giving them grace. If you have decided to forgive your husband for lying to you about how much money he spent on a new set of golf clubs, but in turn you "punish" him by going out and spending the same amount (or more!) on new shoes and clothes, that is not grace. That is manipulation and is more egregious than the original crime committed by your husband. If there is one thing God doesn't like, it's double talk. You must do what you say and follow through with it; otherwise you have made a false promise and shown that you cannot be trusted to move to the next stage of your life that has been laid ahead before you. Grace is hard enough in its own right, but then you throw mercy on top of it, and, whew, that's exhausting. I still struggle with this each day in so many aspects of my life, but I am at least now cognizant of when I need to exhibit grace and mercy, even if it takes time to get there. Self-awareness is more than half the battle.

One of the easiest traps to fall into when going through a rough season, at least for me, is the "Woe is me, how could you do this to me, God" trap. We are so entrenched in what is going wrong for us at that particular moment that we totally dismiss or throw out the amazing things that happen to us each day. To our defense, most of us go through gut-wrenching trials in our lives where it feels like every breath we take becomes harder and more labored and we wonder if we can even live to see another day. I would be lying if I said I didn't have thoughts of whether I could live my life without my husband. We have hearts and emotions. It happens. A few times during my separation and eventual divorce, I would give myself one day to cry and feel sorry for myself, but the next day, I had to put on my big girl pants, throw the box of Kleenex away, put on some clothes other than sweatpants, and live my life. Thankfully, I also had a job and a nine-year-old son to take care of, so it wasn't all about me. My son wouldn't understand why mommy couldn't get out of bed to take him to school or feed him and I doubt his school would have understood either. This is where gratitude comes in. While grace and mercy are difficult because it means sucking up your pride and hurt feelings to be nice to the person who has caused you the pain in the first place, gratitude is all about perspective and outlook. Sure, my husband left me with a mortgage, kid, and medical bills from my surgery and so on and so on. But, I also had a roof over my head because of that mortgage, and I have a son who is one of the best things that has ever happened to me (which I wouldn't have without my husband) and I have a new knee that has allowed me to feel like a real person again. Oh, and did I mention that I still wake up each morning with a job to go to and a car to get me to work? There are many verses in the Bible that describe this very situation and why God allows bad things to happen, even when it seems to contradict everything else you have learned. It may not be apparent immediately, it might not make any sense at all, and it might not become clear for many years to come, but there is a reason for the trial and the pain. It may be that there is something about you that needs to change, and as hard as He has tried to steer you in the right direction, you just didn't listen. I know I fall into that category. It could also mean that where you are or who you are with is not in line with the greater plan that He has for your life. You know the old saying "addition by subtraction?" There are simple things in your life that you need protecting from that are either hurting you, will eventually hurt you, or are holding you captive and complacent. I promise to write a follow-up book in forty years to let you know what situation He was saving me from, although I hope it doesn't take nearly that long!

Unfortunately, our lack of gratitude for the life we have is not driven by our desire to have more or be more; it is driven by our desire to keep up with and compete with others. We are more concerned with what people will think once they find out our marriage is on the rocks. What will they think if we have to downsize the house because we can no longer afford the mortgage? We also fear that we aren't successful enough if we haven't checked the boxes of the things that a person is supposed to have at certain points in our lives. It took me until I was forty to finally get a position where I am directly managing other consultants and I'm still not a manager; I'm a glorified supervisor. I could wallow in self-pity because God is holding me back from climbing the corporate ladder or I could be grateful that He has provided me with a good paying job to take care of my family while He helps me work out this dream to be an author.

It's all about perspective, and if you don't have it, you never will. I heard someone say, "Instead of comparing yourself to others that have more than you, find someone who has it worse than you and make their day." Imagine if we all lived our lives like that instead of stepping all over each other to make ourselves feel better. How about we turn it around and make someone else feel better while we make ourselves feel better? Perspective.

I will admit, as I read more and more scripture and listened to sermons from my pastor as well as others, I was a bit conflicted by some lessons that seemed to contradict many of the adages I was taught growing up. One of the more confusing ideas for me was around pride and humility. As we all heard growing up, "I'm so proud of you," whether it came after you learned how to use the potty for the first time and tie your shoes or graduate from college. Or, "You should be so proud of yourself," when we didn't feel so great about something we had done, but others admired our determination to finish the task. It took me many years to accept kudos from others for things I had accomplished; I didn't want the accolades or I didn't think I had done it well enough to warrant the praises. Pride is also one of the seven deadly sins. Wait, what? It took me sitting down and digging into the word pride much more deeply than I had ever studied a single, one-syllable word. As I researched different methods of Bible study, I learned that in order to digest and fully comprehend the meanings of scripture in the time, place, and context of the passage, you must look at how a word is being used in different ways. Not to seem factitious, but even the word THE can take on many different connotations depending on how, when, and with whom it is being used. Reading comprehension was always my strongest weakness on the SAT and other standardized tests, so this one took some focus and open-mindedness.

Pride in the sense of being sinful relates to being boastful, feeling that you are better than others and stepping on others good works anytime the opportunity arises. Vain and self-centered come to mind, and I'm sure we can all think of someone who fits the description. And, well, if you can't think of someone, it might be you! This is where humility comes in. The word humble is used fifty-six times in the Bible, most notably in James 4:6 (NIV), "But he gives us more grace. That is why Scripture says: "God opposes the Proud but shows favor to the Humble." Continued in verse 10, "Humble yourselves before the Lord and he will lift you up." Simply speaking, God wants us to show our vulnerability, our need for Him in our lives. We wake in the morning, get in our car, and drive to work because of His grace. I am writing this book because of His grace. One miniscule change in details yesterday or a few years ago and I could be living on the streets or, worse, I could have died of cancer or in a car accident. We are so content to live each day oblivious to the fact that we are given enough grace to get us through that very day, no more, no less. You can be as proud and selfish as you want, but it could all be gone tomorrow, in the blink of an eye. Then what? Will you be able to stand at the gates and hear the words, "Well done, my good and faithful servant," or will you be too busy patting yourself on the back that you will not be able to receive and return the loving embrace we all are waiting for at the end of our earthly journey?

"Faith is taking the first step before God reveals the second." Faith is one of those words that rolls right off your tongue, taking virtually no effort to enunciate. But living and acting in faith takes a Herculean effort that most never master because of the forces and circumstances stacked against us as human beings. Faith means turning your life over to someone other than yourself, without knowing why, without knowing the outcome, and without needing your help. I will admit, when I heard others talk about "letting go and letting God," I thought that was just a cute little saying that some marketing genius put on a bumper sticker or a journaling notebook to appeal to our sense of blaming someone else for the misfortunes in our lives. When I ultimately gave in and allowed God to work in me while I was working on me, I began to understand and feel what faith is and how it is working in my life.

This very book is an example of my own stepping out in faith. I have conjured up so many perceived risks in my mind about writing a book, whether it will get published, whether people will actually buy it and read it, and whether people will think I'm crazy or over-dramatic when they read my story. The secret ingredient to getting me closer to the finish line is faith, faith that whatever the purpose is for my sharing, His will be done. I have grown to believe that my experiences were handcrafted, laid out before me for this very reason. Now, it wasn't easy for me to get here; it took a bit of kicking and screaming and pouting, but I'm here. And I'm here because this isn't about me. It never was about me. Someone needs to hear me say that through all the struggles in my life, I am still alive. Someone is longing to find someone they can relate to because they question their purpose in life and don't even know if they want to continue living. Someone needs to know they are not alone. Even when I was going through my divorce, thinking God was listening to me, waiting for Him to answer my prayers to stop the divorce proceedings, when my worst fears became reality, I closed my eyes and said, "I trust you, Lord." I trust that He will turn my messes into a message and my trials into triumphs.

CHAPTER 18

Trust the Process

As cliché as it sounds, life is like one big five-thousand-piece puzzle. In the store (or these days, on Amazon), the picture on the box is so perfect, picturesque, and it seems like it would be relaxing to put together as a hobby. But once at home with the pieces all strewn around the table, some falling on the floor, the dog chewing a rogue piece that wandered off, it takes a little longer than anticipated. You search and search for the first two or three pieces to find their partners and then you just know it will take off from there. But then the phone rings, your kids come home from school, dinner isn't going to cook itself, and the next thing you know the puzzle is back in the box to be completed at another time, a better time, a more convenient time. It took me forty years to begin to put the pieces together, but once I got the outside and corner edges constructed, the inside started to organize itself much more easily and I could see the beginnings of a beautiful finished picture. My puzzle is certainly far from finished, but I'm so close that I can't take the pieces apart and start all over again; I will persist until I succeed. To quit is to abandon necessary action. I have never been a quitter and I am not about to start now.

A few months before this current season in my life, I had started thinking more seriously about my purpose and what I wanted to be when I grow up. I have often felt moved to teach in some way, but after my stint as a substitute teacher, I knew it wasn't going to be in a high school setting! About a year ago, it hit me that my purpose is to serve. Now, what that meant at the time, I wasn't sure. I was already on the board of a nonprofit; I volunteered for several other organizations. What or who else am I meant to serve? Since that time, I have learned the many different interpretations of being a "servant" how they come to fruition in the unique settings I encounter.

I make that sound so easy, like I just woke up one day and said, "I am supposed to serve and this is how I'm going to do it." Trust me, it happened nowhere near that easily and I still have arguments with myself over and over questioning whether I heard something correctly. The biggest obstacle that I continue to face, and many others struggle with, despite this "feeling" that I know what I am meant to do is fear, fear of the unknown, fear of failure, fear of embarrassment, and fear of fear. I have always been afraid of losing, I mean really losing. I don't like to lose any type of competitive activity, but that's just pride, not fear. The losing I fear is where I have absolutely no way to control the outcome and nothing I can do or say will change it. Losing my job for the first time was one of the most crushing blows to my ego because I had never been told I wasn't good enough to do my job. There was no way for me to turn it around and show them that they had made a mistake because I was fired. I didn't get the chance at redemption, and as I'm sure you have learned, I like to prove people wrong. When my husband left me, that feeling of losing and failure came rushing back. I just knew I could fix whatever it was that needed to be fixed, but I didn't get that chance; it was out of my hands. I fear losing when I am given a task that has no end goal, no timeline, no measure of success. When I know what the culmination of my work is supposed to produce and I just have to get to that outcome, I feel much more secure in what I am doing. The end is always in sight, although I may have to course-correct or change my methods of getting there, but I can see the big obnoxious, gold trophy waiting on the winner's stand at the finish line.

This book evokes a little bit of fear in me. I know that I am supposed to share my story with others to motivate and encourage those who find themselves in helpless or hopeless situations, but I still don't know what the end of this journey looks like. Have you ever been driving late on a dark night, maybe after a small rain shower in the summertime, and the fog is so thick you can barely see what's in front of you? And when you put your high beams on, expecting them to cut straight through the mist like a hot knife through, instead you are met with an even thicker shield of gray and white clouds? That is what writing this book feels like to me, at times. What's different is that I am embracing that smokescreen as more of a curtain, the kind of curtain that usually means there is something you have been waiting behind it. There is a surprise behind that curtain that if I saw or already knew what was there, I might look right on past the beautiful, amazing things that are happening around me because I am so excited for the ending. When you are on that dark, foggy road, when you finally reach your destination, driving ever so slowly as not to miss it, you suddenly see it!, the mailbox with the address that you've been looking for! And then, you breathe a sigh of relief; the color in your knuckles starts to come back as you let go of the steering wheel you have tightly been clinging onto; you appreciate making it to your destination in one piece.

I am not an author, and I have never pretended to be one. I have journaled through tough spots in my life for many years, but I wouldn't consider any of that "novel-worthy" to say the least. But I enjoy writing. I enjoy sharing my thoughts with others and sometimes I need get it out of my head to wrap my head around what I'm thinking about. Writing is easy for me. In college, I would prefer to write a twenty-page paper on any subject in place of a five-question multiple choice test. I am a horrible test taker, especially when it comes to topics I have no interest in. But I can spout off for twenty pages about anything and make you believe I am an expert even if I have no clue what on earth I'm talking about. My dad used to tell me I got the right degree when I was in college, my BS. Some might take that as a backhanded remark, but coming from my dad, who had his own BS without stepping foot into a college classroom, those were pretty high praises!

I have heard a few different quotes about how God comes into people's lives in exceptional ways to drive them to where He has meant for them to be. Most times people find themselves completely off course, with no idea how they arrived at the final destination. "He doesn't call the qualified. He qualifies the called." The first time I heard that, I thought, "Qualified for what? And who is He calling?" Although I have been thinking of this book for many years, I was not qualified to write it ten or even five years ago, not qualified, meaning being a published writer with articles and other books to my name, qualified in the sense that before I can talk about some things, I have to go through some things. There is no message without a mess. There is no testimony without a test. Now, I am more than qualified to share my life with the world, to show what He has done for me and how He is using me to show His glory. I have spent the last ten years of my life as a forecaster/analyst, dissecting data for insights and knowledge through numbers. Why would you want to read a book about anything from an analyst? If you didn't know what this book was about, you might assume that I'm going to write a book about the analysis of the retail environment and its impact on the overall socioeconomic landscape of our global financial system. Nah, I don't have any clue what that means, but if you heard that an analyst was writing a book, you might think that's what I'm going to write about. But if you heard bits and pieces of my story and you knew a little about some of the tragedies and cycle of misfortunes I have experienced, you then may be intrigued to hear what I have to say and believe that I have a platform to stand on to say it. You can trust what I'm saying because you know I went through it; I'm not making any of this up; it's not a work of fiction.

My calling to serve means that I support others who are less fortunate than me, those who have a passion for something but need help in honing that passion, those who have lost their way and need help to find faith and hope again, and those who just need to know that someone else is going through something. I have dreams, but my dreams involve raising others up to reach their dreams. I draw my passion from others' energy. At earlier points in my life, I would have considered myself an introvert because I enjoyed being by myself and I felt more comfortable being alone. Now, I would say that I have flipped that script and I do more reflecting out than I do reflecting in. I no longer enter a situation trying to figure out, "What's in it for me?" I was admittedly selfish when I first entered the real world because I was always searching for the next promotion, the next raise, the next opportunity to make a name for myself. And I took pride in being called a go-getter. Now it's about helping make others better and reaching back to pull someone else with me as I progress, teaching them the things to avoid that I was not successfully able to do.

We are supposed to learn from others; we were never meant to know everything about everything. The constant striving for perfection does nothing but make you tired, lonely, stressed, and frustrated. Bringing others on your spiritual, professional, or personal journey means that you have someone who is counting on you, but you also have an invested partner who allows you to take a break and lean on them if you come to a bridge that you just can't quite conquer on your own. There is more than enough success in the world for us all to have a piece. And this isn't about socialism or asking the one percent of the world to simply stop making money when they reach a certain level of wealth. This is about happiness and finding YOUR passion, YOUR inheritance, YOUR lot in life. There is nothing that says that your being successful or fulfilled in your endeavors is directly related to another's disappointments or failures. Our victories are not measured on a scale that teeters and totters back and forth depending on the performance of someone else's dreams on the other side. In fact, it should be just the opposite. As you rise, others should rise. Not because they are following in your footsteps and riding your coattails, but because you have set an example for someone who is watching what you are doing. That could be a co-worker, a neighbor, your children, or even a stranger halfway around the world who has never even met you, but has heard your story. Success begets success, it does not hinder it, and when we all stop trying to one-up each other and instead learn from and with others, we will reap the benefits and harvest the good we have sown.

CHAPTER 19

My Next Forty Years

If you don't take away anything else from my testimony about the good things God has built from the broken pieces of my journey, please remember this. It is never too late to start over and be where you want to be, be who you were meant to be, and be who God has sent you to be. It may take a little longer to figure out than most, but here I am writing a book at the age of forty-one after spending the last fifteen years in the data-driven world of analytics. Did you know that Colonel Sanders was close to seventy years old when he started Kentucky Fried Chicken?

It took me forty years of practice to get where I am today, to adequately prepare myself through the spiritual and physical battles I have endured on my journey. In all my years of athletics, there is one thing I have learned that I can still use in my current life. Practice does no good if you are practicing the incorrect form or with improper equipment. You wouldn't go to basketball practice with a golf club or a football helmet, would you? Practice is also worthless if you don't use what you have learned when you get in the game. The same is true for the way we live our lives. If you go through and successfully complete difficult stages in your life, but then you go right back to the unhealthy habits you had before the trial, then the pain you suffered was worthless, null and void.

One of the first natural reactions to something gone awry in our lives is to ask, "Why me?" Some go ask far to say, "If God is so good, why would He let this happen?" I'll tell you why. He has plans for your life, plans that you can't even dream of, plans that, unless He removes someone or something from your life, you will not fully comprehend or obey and you will continue to lead the mediocre life you have been living. Trust me, God brought me to my knees by literally taking them out from under me, how's that for irony and symbolism? He had to bring me down in order to build me back up. The pain that manifested itself over twenty years ago was the jumping off point to the twists, turns, U-turns, and wrong turns that delivered me to where I am right now.

My college basketball coach, known for her very pointed way of getting your best out of you, always told me to stop worrying about her yelling at me for doing something wrong. She said it was when she stops yelling, stops pushing me to better that I should worry, because it means she has given up on me. I feel the same is true in our relationship with God. He will never give up on me, but He wouldn't put me through the trials I have endured if He didn't think I could handle it. If He didn't think I had the potential to serve a greater purpose on this earth, He would let me go through my life on auto-pilot, settling for mediocrity, never dreaming to do extraordinary things that I couldn't even imagine. It would mean that He believes I have reached the peak of my existence and I will continue to sit where I am because of my refusal to obey Him during those trials. I am not one to let others down and I am not about to start now.

Although this is the end of this season, my story is still being written. Lucky for me, I have already been assured of one thing, victory. The trials may get tougher from here, my adversaries may get smarter and stronger and attack me with formations I have never prepared myself for, but I am guaranteed victory. I know that because I have moved up to a new level, the expectations have also been raised, but I have proven to be an obedient servant as I continue to carry out the purpose I have been created for.

"For I know the plans I have for you," declares the Lord, *"plans to prosper you and not to harm you, plans to give you hope and a future."* **Jeremiah 29: 11**

My life began at forty, and the best is yet to come.

ABOUT THE AUTHOR

Tezlyn Reardon is the author of *Forty Years of Practice*, her first published work she hopes is the first of many. An avid reader from an early age, Tezlyn communicates best through her authentic, raw writing style coupled with life-defining experiences, allowing her to mentor and guide others in similar situations. Her vision is not only to encourage others to embrace the difficult, sometimes gut-wrenching circumstances we will all encounter in our lives but to also motivate individuals of all ages to follow their passions and dreams, no matter what purpose in pain, as long as we are still breathing, we all have a purpose.

Tezlyn Reardon is a mother, daughter, niece, friend, teammate, and servant. When not spending time recording her experiences to break into the writing game, she is chasing down her nine-year-old son, Tyson, who is being chased by their one-year-old black lab, Hopper. She lives with her two boys in Pickerington, Ohio, where she is a faithful fan of THE Ohio State University Buckeyes. She also enjoys following her alma mater, the University of Massachusetts Minutemen in all sports and educational successes.